Buddhist Civilization in Tibet

Buddhist Civilization in Tibet

Tulku Thondup Rinpoche

Routledge & Kegan Paul
New York and London

First published in 1987 by
Routledge & Kagan Paul Inc.
in association with Methuen Inc.
29 West 35th Street, New Tork, NY 10001

Published in the UK by
Routledge & Kegan Paul Ltd.
11 New Fetter Lane, London EC4P 4EE

Set in Plantin, 10 on 12pt
by Pentacor Ltd, High Wycombe, Bucks
and printed in Great Britain
by T.J. Press Ltd, Padstow, Cornwall

Buddhayara Series: II

Library of Congress Cataloging in Publication Data

Thondup, Tulku.
Buddhist civilization in Tibet.

(Buddhayana series; 2)
Includes index.
1. Buddhism—China—Tibet. I Title.
II. Series.
BQ7604.T47 1987 294.3'923'09515 87-4493
British Library CIP Data also available
ISBN 0–7102–1087–6

CONTENTS

PREFACE

This book contains two essays which I wrote some ten years ago. The first, 'The Development of Buddhism in Tibet', is a brief account of the history of the four major Buddhist schools in Tibet. It includes a description of their doctrines and monastic institutions. These four schools are the Nyingma (the Ancient One), which follows the Old Tantras (those tantras translated into Tibetan before the eleventh century AD), the Kagyud, Sakya, and Gelug which follow the New Tantras (those tantras which were translated during and after the eleventh century AD). The account which I have given in this essay is the traditional version of the history of Buddhism in Tibet as it appears in Tibetan historical texts.

The second essay is a brief outline of Tibetan literature. It classifies the works on various subjects, secular and religious. I have included the names of only a few major literary works as examples of each category.

I wrote this book while I was a Visiting Scholar at the Center for the Study of World Religions at Harvard University. I am grateful for the joint sponsorship of the Center and of Michael Baldwin and the other members of Buddhayana. I am thankful to Harold Talbott for editing the essays. For their help at various stages of the book, my gratitude goes to Dan and Sybil Jorgenson, Eric Jacobson, Martha Hamilton and Tenzin Parsons.

NOTE ON TRANSLITERATION

I have capitalized the root-letters (Ming gZhi) of each word in the transliterated Tibetan in order to ensure a correct reading. When the root-letters are not capitalized, it is possible to confuse two entirely different words. For example, 'Gyi' means 'of', while the meaning of 'gYi' is 'lynx'. Many technical terms are rendered in either transliteration or phonetic spelling followed by transliteration. Nearly all the titles of texts are listed in transliteration as they will be useful mainly for scholarly reference.

INTRODUCTION

The extraordinary characteristic of Buddhism is its multiple ways of training in order to suit the capacity, nature and wishes of individual followers. It is a training which has the power to touch the hearts of people while it deals with the mind at its root through a common sense approach. It has the effect of transmuting every aspect of one's life, livelihood and perceptions as the means of spiritual training. Buddhism never propagates itself by forced conversion or conversion for the sake of material benefits. It encourages not blind faith but acceptance as a result of understanding and appreciation. The Buddha said:

> "Monks and scholars should
> Analyze my teachings well,
> As gold is tested by
> melting, cutting and polishing.
> Only then adopt them, but not for
> (the sake of showing me) respect."

During its twenty-five-century history, Buddhism crossed the borders of many countries and sailed to different continents bearing the light of love and compassion, becoming a native and humanistic faith for both royal courts and common folk. Buddhism is characterized by compassion, which is the foundation of its training. The Buddha said:

> "The teachings of Buddhism are distinguished by compassion."

Buddhism in Tibet is a tradition in which all the major ways of Buddhist training such as the Hinayāna (including Theravada), Mahāyāna, and Vajrayāna teachings are preserved and are being thoroughly studied, practiced and realized by a great number of followers. There are different schools and traditions of Buddhism in Tibet. Each emphasizes particular scriptures, traditions and lineages, but they all embody the training in full. Every phase of the life of a traditional Tibetan is based on and modeled by Buddhism.

ETHICAL DISCIPLINES OF BUDDHISM

Buddhist training mainly emphasizes disciplining one's own mind. As mind is the forerunner and essential part of all activities, if one's mind is virtuous, all one's physical and vocal actions will turn out to be peaceful, virtuous, and a source of happiness and enlightenment for others. In the *Dhammapada* Buddha said:

> "Mind is the forerunner of all phenomena.
> They are mind made, and mind is the chief.
> If with a pure mind one speaks or acts,
> Then happiness follows like a shadow
> which never departs."

For those who become ordained and those who remain lay followers, the way of entering into Buddhism is to accept the 'three jewels' as the refuges followed by observance of the precepts. First, one accepts or goes for refuge to the 'three jewels.' One accepts the Buddha as the teacher who guides in the path to enlightenment, the Dharma or Buddhism as the path to be followed and the Sangha or Buddhist community as the companion who supports one along the journey. To make a strong determination and to commit oneself to the training is the entrance into Buddhism since without commitment no serious project will ever be accomplished.

Two categories of elementary precepts are observed by lay devotees. The first is the 'five precepts.'

(1) Abstaining from destroying life
(2) Abstaining from taking what is not given
(3) Abstaining from sexual misconduct
(4) Abstaining from false speech
(5) Abstaining from the causes of intoxication and heedlessness

The second category is the 'ten virtuous deeds', which king Srong-tsen Gam-po (AD617–698) promulgated in Tibet as the common law of the land. Since then it has remained as the ethical guide of Tibetan civilization:

Three virtuous deeds of the body:
- (1) Refraining from killing
- (2) Refraining from stealing
- (3) Refraining from sexual misconduct

Four virtuous deeds of speech:
- (1) Refraining from lying
- (2) Refraining from slander
- (3) Refraining from harsh words
- (4) Refraining from senseless talk

Three virtuous deeds of the mind:
- (1) Refraining from covetousness
- (2) Refraining from ill will
- (3) Refraining from wrong view

THE WAYS OF TRAINING

Of the many ways available, seriously involved Buddhists who seek the attainment of the goal must pursue a way which suits their nature and ability. Today the Buddhist teachings have developed into three major traditions, *Hinayāna, Mahāyāna* and *Vajrayāna* or *Tantra*. Tibetans are followers of *Mahāyāna,* and there is no traditional Tibetan who has not also been initiated into *Vajrayāna* training. Tibetans also study and practice *Hinayāna* teachings, which in many ways constitute the foundation of Buddhist training. A highly capable individual will even be able to train in all three *Yānas* simultaneously. He trains himself physically in *Hinayāna* teachings such as living a celibate life in solitude. Mentally he trains in *Mahāyāna* teachings such as compassion, and assumes the responsibility of serving people directly. His innermost training is in the esoteric teachings of *Vajrayāna* through the pure perception of seeing everything as the form, speech and mind of the enlightened divinities and dwelling in the wisdom, the union of bliss, clarity and freedom from conceptions.

HINAYĀNA

Its main emphasis is on physical discipline such as dwelling in solitude, simple livelihood and celibacy in order to avoid encountering the emotions and the conditions which make them arise. Hinayānists meditate on the five aggregates and all the knowable objects through the insight of the 'four noble truths' (a'Phags-Pa'i bDen-Pa bZhi): the truth of suffering, which characterizes the whole of existence; the truth of the source of suffering, which is desire, 'thirst' accompanied by all other mental defilements; the truth of cessation, which is the emancipation from suffering and its causes; and the truth of the path of cessation, which is the contemplation on the meaning of the four noble truths with the 'thirty-seven aspects of enlightenment,' in particular the 'noble eightfold path.' After completing the first four paths, Hinayānists attain the fifth path, that of the Arhat (Sagehood), the Destroyer of Foes or the Worthy One.

MAHĀYĀNA

Its main emphasis is on disciplining the mental attitudes, notably the developing of a compassionate mind. Mahāyānists use contemplations on virtuous attitudes and meditative absorptions as antidotes to the mental defilements. In their training they use compassion as the antidote to anger, awareness that suffering and impermanence are the nature of cyclic existence as the antidote to desire, and reflection on interdependent causation and meditation on emptiness as the antidote to ignorance. They devote their lives to bearing the responsibility of serving others without any self-interest through the course of training on the 'six perfections' (*Phar-Phyin Drug*.) These are the perfections of generosity, moral discipline, patience, perseverance, contemplation and wisdom. They meditate on the 'thirty-seven aspects of enlightenment' (*Byang-Chub Kyi Ch'os Sum-Chu rTsa-bDun*)and progress through the 'five paths' (*Lam-lNga*) and 'ten stages' (*Sa-bChu*) of attainment for numerous eons until they attain the fully enlightened state, Buddhahood.

1 Path of accumulation (*Tshogs-Lam*):
In the three levels of this path one practices three sets of four trainings in the 'thirty-seven aspects of enlightenment.' In the 'small

level' (*Ch'ung-Ngu*) one reflects on the meaning of the 'four noble truths' through the 'four awarenesses' (*Dran-Pa Nye-Bar bZhag-Pa*):

(a) Awareness of the body; for contemplation on the truth of suffering, since the body is the result and also the main cause of miseries.

(b) Awareness of feeling; for the truth of the source of suffering, the emotional defilements, since feeling is the source of craving, which is the chief of defilements.

(c) Awareness of mind; for the truth of cessation, since in order for it to cease, it is necessary to analyse the mind, which is the basis of concepts of self.

(d) Awareness of phenomena; for the truth of the path, since it is the basis of apprehension of cyclic existence and cessation of suffering.

In the 'mediocre level' (*a'Bring*) one trains in the 'four perfect purifications' (*Yan-Dag sPong-Ba*): they are the training in the vigor produced as a result of training in the fourfold awareness:

(a) Not to generate any unvirtuousness which has not been generated.

(b) To abandon all the unvirtuousness which has been generated.

(c) To generate virtues which have not been generated.

(d) To increase the virtues which have been generated.

In the 'great level' (*Ch'en-Po*) one trains in the 'four miraculous contemplations' (*rDzu-a'Phrul Gyi rKang-Pa*). As the effect of vigor, these are the means of training in one-pointed contemplations of mind: (a) admiration, (b) diligence, (c) mind and (d) analysis (wisdom).

2 **Path of application (sByor-Lam):**

In the four levels of this path one trains in ten of the 'thirty-seven aspects of enlightenment.' In the first two levels of this path, known as 'heat' (*Drod*) and 'climax' (*rTse-Mo*), one trains in the 'five faculties' (*dBang-Po*), the means enabling one to generate liberative virtues: (a) faith, (b) diligence, (c) awareness, (d) contemplation, and (e) wisdom.

In the 'forbearance' (*nZod-Pa*) and 'supreme (mundane) realization' (*Ch'os-mCh'og*), the last two levels, one trains in the 'five powers' (*sTobs*), in which faith, etc., the antidotes, are more powerful and the defilements are weaker than in the case of the 'four faculties': (a) faith, (b) diligence, (c) contemplation, and (e) wisdom.

3 Path of insight (*mThong-Lam*):
In this path one trains in the 'seven branches of the path of enlightenment' (*Byang-Ch'ub Kyi Lam Yan-Lag brGyad*) of the 'thirty-seven aspects of enlightenment.' These are the training in and support of wisdom free from conceptualizations, the realization of suchness, the ultimate nature of the 'four noble truths.' By realizing the path of insight one attains the first of the 'ten stages' (*Sa-bChu*). The 'seven branches of the path of enlightenment' are:
(a) Awareness; unforgetfulness of the insight realization.
(b) Discrimination; wisdom which destroys the characteristics of the concept of self.
(c) Diligence; joyfulness in the efforts which apply to the realization.
(d) Joy; joyfulness in contemplation and realization of the truth.
(e) Pliancy; physical and mental maturation of bliss without emotions.
(f) Contemplation; contemplating one-pointedly on the state free from emotions.
(g) Equanimity; remaining in the nature free from emotions.

These are meditations on and for developing the realization which is or leads to the freedom from suffering, detachment from the source of suffering, dwelling in the cessation of suffering and contemplation on the path of cessation.

4 Path of meditation (*bsGom-Lam*):
In this path one trains on the 'noble eightfold path' (*a'Phags-Lam Yan-Lag brGyad*). In this context, the 'noble eightfold path' is for progressing and perfecting the realization which one has attained in the 'path of insight.' It consists of contemplations on the ultimate nature (*Ch'os-Nyid*) of the 'four noble truths.' This path has nine levels, and by perfecting each level one attains the last nine of the 'ten stages.' The 'noble eightfold path' is:
(a) Right view; realization of the wisdom which has been attained.
(b) Right thought; thoughts of virtues and of teaching one's realization to others.
(c) Right speech; pure from the four unvirtuous types of speech.
(d) Right action; pure from the three physical unvirtuous deeds.
(e) Right livelihood; pure from wrong livelihood.

(f) Right effort; diligence in purifying the defilements.

(g) Right awareness; contemplation with unforgetfulness and purification of secondary emotions such as laxity and elation.

(h) Right contemplation; through the fourth absorption dispelling the obstructions to attainment of the extraordinary virtues.

The first two concern wisdom, the next three moral discipline to generate faith in others, and the last three contemplation to purify the obstructions.

5 **Path of no more training (*Mi-Slob Lam*):**
After completion of the four paths and ten stages and the abandoning of the two obscurations, the emotional and intellectual obscurations with their traces, one attains the fifth path, Buddhahood, which possesses the 'Four Bodies' and 'Five Wisdoms.'

The four bodies (*sKu-bZhi*) are:

(a) The Natural (Absolute) body (*Ngo-Bo Nyid-sKu*); it is the body of twofold ultimate purity: pure from the origin and pure from adventitious defilements.

(b) The Truth body (*Ch'os-sKul*) is the wisdom body, the aspect of the knowledge possessing twenty-one sets of uncontaminated attainments.

(c) The Enjoyment body (*Longs-sKul*) is the ultimate form body of the Buddhas with thirty-two major and eighty minor marks, possessing five certainties.

(d) The Manifested body (*sPrul-sKu*) is the ceaseless manifestations in various ordinary forms for the benefit of every possible being.

The five wisdoms (*Ye-Shes lNga*) of the Buddhas:

(a) The Wisdom of the Ultimate Sphere (*Ch'os-dByings Ye-Shes*) is the omnipresent wisdom inseparable from the ultimate sphere. This is the basis on which it is called the Natural Body and Truth Body.

(b) Mirror-like Wisdom (*Me-Long Ye-Shes*) is like a reflection in a mirror, it knows all clearly but has no concept of subject and object. It is the source of the next three wisdoms and the basis on which the Enjoyment body is so named.

(c) The Wisdom of Equanimity (*mNyam-Nyid Ye-Shes*) is the dwelling in equanimity by going beyond the extremes of cyclic existence and peace, and the manifesting of appropriate Buddha-bodies for all equally.

(d) Discriminative Wisdom (*Sor-rTog Ye-Shes*) is the wisdom knowing all without error, and showering Dharma rain upon all.

(e) The Wisdom of Accomplishment (*Bya-Grub Ye-Shes*) is the accomplishment of all the possible benefits of the universe through the enlightened action of body, speech and mind of the Buddhas.

VAJRAYĀNA

In *Vajrayāna* or *Tantric* (esoteric) training, the main emphasis is on pure perception and the transformation of every aspect of perception and life into meditative training through esoteric skills. After having been initiated into the esoteric wisdom, one trains in the 'two stages' of practice: the 'development stage' (*bsKyed-Rim*) and the 'perfection stage' (*rDzogs-Rim*):

(a) In the development stage, one visualizes and realizes all the forms in the universe; beings and the world as the forms of enlightened deities and their Buddha-fields, sounds and speech as the sacred communications or transmissions of enlightened speech, and thoughts as the virtues and wisdom minds of Buddhahood.

(b) In the perfection stage, one trains in and realizes the innate wisdom, the wisdom of the union of bliss, clarity and freedom from concepts produced through the process of training on the fourfold bliss, and so on, by exerting the skillful means of channels, energy and essence of one's *vajra*-body.

Through the training on the union of the two stages one attains Buddhahood, with four bodies and five wisdoms, in this very lifetime or in the next few lifetimes. In *Vajrayāna* one trains on the 'thirty-seven aspects of enlightenment' and progresses through the 'five paths' and 'ten stages' of attainment. In this *yāna* the practice on the 'thirty-seven aspects of enlightenment' applies to the training on the two stages. These aspects are practiced by seeing, symbolizing and transforming the respective virtues of the path and result as well as the structures of the *maṇḍalas* of the Buddha-fields and different manifestations of the

Buddhas as the 'thirty-seven aspects of enlightenment.' Also one practices on the mental and phenomenal entities by transforming them as the means of training or by realizing their ultimate nature as it is. All the scriptures of different *yānas* of Buddhist teachings are translated and preserved in Tibetan. And fortunately the Buddhism of Tibet is still a living tradition of vigorous scholarship and practice leading to enlightenment.

Key political and religious figures in Tibetan history

FOUNDERS OF RELIGIOUS SCHOOLS AND TRANSLATORS	KINGS
2nd CENTURY	
	Nyathri Tsenpo *enthroned in 127 BC.* *First king of Tibet.* *Founded Chogyal Dynasty.*
5th CENTURY	
	Lhatho Thori Nyentsen *Brought first Buddhist scriptures and religious objects into Tibet in AD 433.*
7th CENTURY Early Spread of the Doctrine, 7th–10th Century AD	
Thonmi Sambhota *First Tibetan Buddhist translator.* *Invented Tibetan script and grammar.*	Srongtsen Gampo (AD617–698) *Directed the development of a written form of Tibetan language.* *Inaugurated Buddhism as the religion of Tibet.*
9th CENTURY	
Padmasambhava *Came from India to establish Buddhism in Tibet.* *Founded Nyingma School.* Śāntarakṣita, Vimalamitra } *Great Indian scholars who visited Tibet* Vairocana Kawa Paltseg, Chogro Lu'i Gyaltshen, Zhang Yeshe De — *Tibetan translators* Ṣurendrabodhi, Śīlendrabodhi, Dānasīla, Jinamitra — *Indian scholars* Ratnarakṣita, Dharmatāśīla, Jñānasena } *Tibetan scholars*	Thrisong Deutsen (AD 790–858) *Invited greatest Indian saints and yogis to teach Buddhism in Tibet.* *Directed construction of Samye monastery.* Thri Ralpachen (866–901) *Assassinated by pro–Bon ministers.*
10th CENTURY	
Nub Chen Sangye Yeshes *Preserved Tantric tradition.* La Chen Gangpa Rabsal *Re-established Vinaya tradition.*	Lang Darma, ruled 901–906 *Persecuted and suppressed Buddhism in Tibet. Assassinated by Lhalung Paldor. End of the Chogyal dynasty.*
10th–13th CENTURIES	
Smṛtijñāna *Last great translator of the earlier spread of the doctrine.*	No central authority (906–1253) *Gradual return of Buddhist practice in central Tibet to the end of the 10th century.*

10th CENTURY Later Spread of the Doctrine 10th–20th centuries AD.

Rinchen Zangpo (958–1051)
First great translator of the later spread of the doctrine.

11th CENTURY

Atīśa (982–1055?) **of India**
Founded Kadam school.

Lha Lama Yeshe Od and Changchub Od,
rulers of western Tibet.

Drogmi Sakya Yeshes (993–1050)
Nagtsho Tshulthrim (1011–?)
} *Great translators*

Marpa (1012–1099)
Founded Kagyud school.
Khon Konchog Gyalpo (1034–1102)
Founded Sakya school.
Ngog Loden Sherab (1059–1109)
A great translator.

13th CENTURY

Drogon Chogyal Phagpa (1235–80).
Given the rulership of Tibet by Kublai Khan of the Yuan dynasty of China in 1253. Sakyapa rule began.

14th CENTURY

Phagtru Changchub Gyaltshen (1302–64).
Overthrew Sakyapa rule in 1349.
Phagtrupa rule began.
Eleven Phagtrupa rulers.

Je Tsongkhapa (1357–1419)
Founded Gelug school.

15th CENTURY

Donyod Dorje
Overthrew Phagtrupa rule in 1435.
Began Ringpungpa rule.
Four Ringpungpa rulers.

16th CENTURY

Tsheten Dorje
Overthrew Ringpungpa rule in 1566.
Began Tsangpa rule.
Three Tsangpa rulers.

17th CENTURY

Gushri Khan, *a Mongolian ruler, defeated Tsangpa ruler in 1646 and gave rulership over Tibet to the 5th Dalai Lama (1617–82). Began rule of the Dalai Lamas.*

PRESENT

14th Dalai Lama (1935–?)
Lives in exile in India.

Key figures in the Nyingma tradition

Early Spread of the Doctrine, 9th and 10th centuries AD

Padmasambhava (9th cent) Śāntarakṣita (9th cent) Vimalamitra (9th cent)	*Came from India to teach Buddhism in Tibet*
Vairochana (9th cent) Kawa Paltseg (9th cent) Chogro Lu'i Gyaltsen (9th cent) Zhang Yeshe De (9th cent)	*Main Tibetan translators among the 108*
Nubchen Sangye Yeshe (9th cent)	*Preserved Tantric tradition*

Later Spread of the Doctrine—started from later half of the 10th century AD

Lachen Gongpa Rabsal (10th cent)	*Re-established/preserved Vinaya in central Tibet.*
Smṛtijñāna (11th cent)	*The last translator of the Old Tantras*

Some of the great Tertons (Dharma treasure discoverers)

Nyangral Nyima Odzer (1124–1192)
Guru Chowang (1212–1270/3)
Rigdzin Goddem (1337–1408)
Sangye Lingpa (1340–1396)
Dorje Lingpa (1346–1405)
Ratna Lingpa (1403–1478)
Padma Lingpa (1450–1521)
Rigdzin Jatshon Nyingpo (1585–1656)
Duddul Dorje (1615–1672)
Lhatsun Namkha Jigmed (1597–1650?)
Terchen Gyurmed Dorje (1646–1714)
Rigdzin Jigmed Lingpa (1729–1798)
Jamyang Khyentse'i Wangpo (1820–1892)
Chogkyur Lingpa (1829–1870)

Some of the great writers

Rongzom Chozang (11th century)
Longchen Rabjam (1308–1363)
Ngari Pema Wanggyal (1487–1542)
Lochen Dharmashri (1654–1717/8)
Paltrul Rinpoche (1808–1887)
Ju Mipham Namgyal (1846–1912)
Third Dodrup Chen (1865–1926)
Zhenphen Chokyi Nangwa (1871–1927)
Khenpo Ngagwang Palzang (1879–1941)

Recent head

Jigtral Yeshe Dorje
the 2nd Dudjom Rinpoche (1904–1987)

Key figures in the Kagyud tradition

MARPA
(1012–1099)
Founded Kagyud School

MILAREPA
(1040–1123)

GAMPOPA
(1079–1153)

Karmapa Dusum Khyenpa (1110–1193)
Founded Karma Kagyud

Phagmo Trupa, Dorje Gyalpo (1110–1170)
Founded Phagtru Kagyud

Wongom Tshulthrim Nyingpo (12th century)

Zhangdarma Trag (1122–?)
Founded Tshalpa Kagyud

Darma Wangchug (12th century)
Founded Barompa Kagyud

Taglung Thangpa Trashi Pal (1142–1210)
Founded Taglung Kagyud

Drikung Kyobpa (1143–1217)
Founded Drigung Kagyud

Tsangpa Gyare (1161–1211)
Founded Drugpa Kagyud

Some of the great writers

Karmapa Rangchung Dorje (1284–1334)
Karmapa Mikyod Dorje (1507–1554)
Kunkhyen Padma Karpo (1527–1592)
Pawo Tsuglag Threngwa (1454–1566)
Situ Tenpa'i Nyinched (1698–?)
Kongtrul Yonten Gyatsho (1813–1899)

Most recent head

Rigpa'i Dorje, the 16th Karmapa (1924–1981)

Regent of Karmapa

The 13th Zharmar Rinpoche (1952–)

Key figures in the Sakya tradition

10th–11th centuries

Khon Konchog Gyalpo (1034–1102)

Built Sakya monastery in 1073 and founded the Sakya school.

11th–12th centuries

Sachen Kunga Nyingpo (1092–1158)

A great scholar and adept.

12th century

Sodnam Tsemo (1142–1182)

A great teacher and sage.

12th–13th centuries

Tragpa Gyaltshen (1147–1216)

A great teacher and ascetic.

Kunga Gyaltshen (1181–1251), Sakya Pandita

The greatest scholar of the Sakya lineage, re-introduced Buddhism in Mongolia.

13th centuries

Droygon Chogyal Phagpa (1234–1280)

Became a preceptor of Kublai Khan of the Yuan dynasty of China, who gave him rule over Tibet in 1253.

He was the first priest ruler of Tibet.

14th–15th centuries

Rongton Shecha Kunrig (1367–1449)

Great scholar who built the Nalentra monastery in Phanpo valley in 1437.

Ngorchen Kunga Zangpo (1382–1456)

Built Ngor E-Wam Choden monastery and founded the Ngor sub-school.

15th–16th centuries

Sakya Chogden (1428–1507)

A great writer.

Go Ranjam Sodnam Senge (1429–1489)

An outstanding writer, scholar and critic, who built the Tanag monastery in Tsang in 1414.

16th century

Tshalchen Losal Gyatsho (1502–1566)

Founded Tshalpa sub-school.

19th century

Khyentse Wangpo (1820–1892)

An important figure in the Rime movement.

Present head

Kunga Thrinle Wangyal, Thri Rinpoche (1945–)

41st holder of the Throne of Sakya.

Key figures in the Gelug tradition

14th century

Je Tsong Khapa, Lobzang Tragpa (1357–1419)
One of the greatest scholars and writers of Tibet.
He built Gaden monastery in 1410, propagated strict monastic disciplines and founded the Gelug school.

14th–15th centuries

Gyaltshab Je (1364–1432)

Khedrub Je (1385–1438)

Chamchen Choje (1354–1435)
Built Sera monastery in 1429.

Jamyang Choje (1379–1449)
Built Drepung monastery in 1419.

Panchen Gedundrub (1391–1474), first Dalai Lama
Built Trashi Lhunpo monastery in 1447.

15th–16th centuries

Jetsun Chokyi Gyaltshen (1469–1546)
Great writer and scholar of Sera monastery.

Panchen Sodnam Tragpa (1478–1554)
Great writer and scholar of Drepung monastery.

16th century

Sodnam Gyatsho (1543–1588), third Dalai Lama
He received the title of Dalai Lama from the Mongol king Altan Khan and he built Kubum (Taer) monastery.

16th–17th centuries

Lobzang Chokyi Gyaltshen (1570–1662)
First Panchen Lama, who is the greatest ritual text compiler of the Gelug school.

17th century

Ngangwang Lobzang Gyatsho (1617–82), fifth Dalai Lama.
He became the spiritual and temporal head of Tibet in 1642.

17th–18th centuries

Lobzang Tenpa'i Gyaltshen (1635–1723), first Jetsun Dampa
He and his incarnations were the highest spiritual and temporal authorities of Mongolia until the revolution.
He built Riwo Gegyeling monastery in Mongolia.

Ngagwang Tsondru (1648–1721), first Jamyang Zhedpa
He built Trashikhyil monastery in Amdo in 1710.

18th century

Changkya Rolpa'i Dorje (1717–1786)

The successive Changkya incarnations were influential teachers in China.

20th century

Tendzin Gyatsho (1935–), the 14th Dalai Lama

Chokyi Gyaltshen (1938–), the 7th Panchen Lama

Present head

Jampal Zhenphen (1921–)

The 98th holder of the Throne of Gaden.

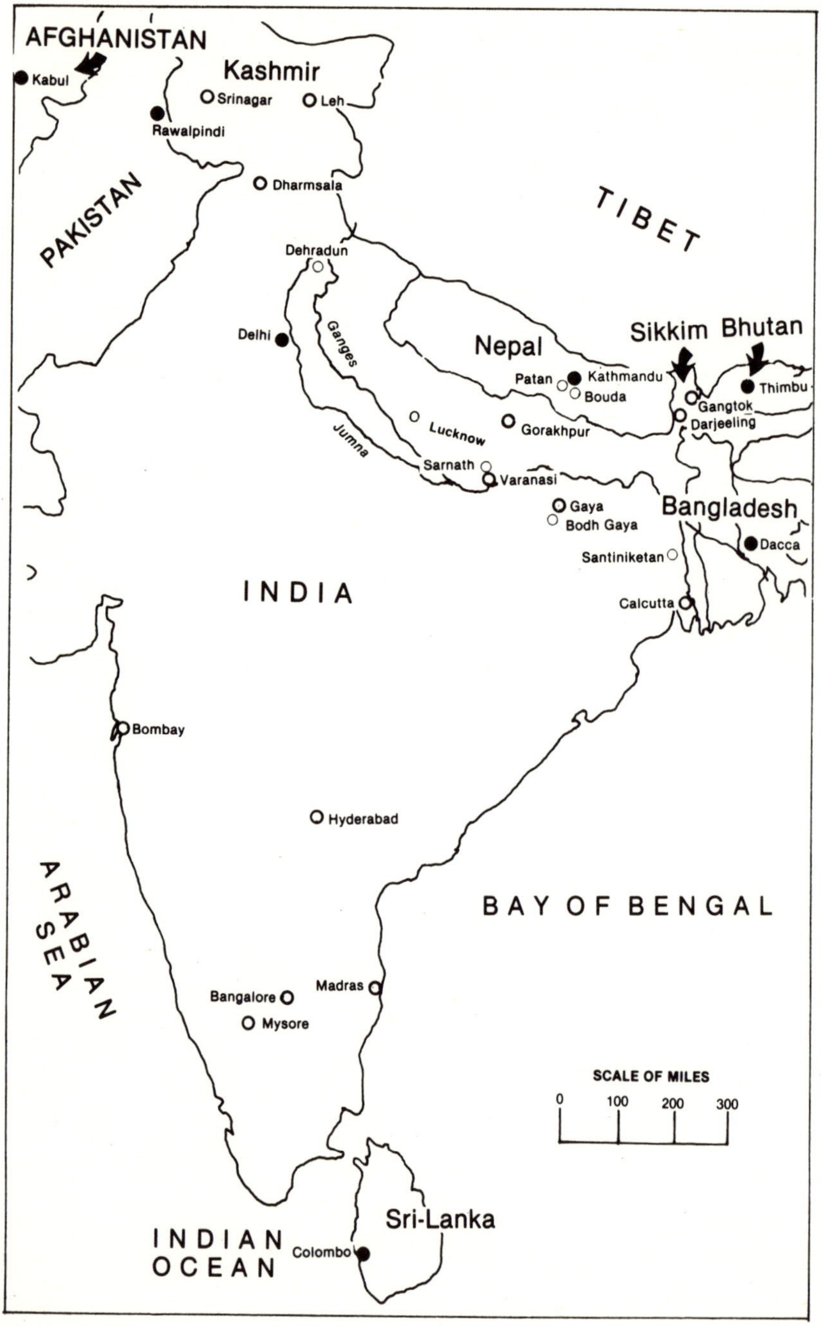
AFGHANISTAN
Kabul
Kashmir
Srinagar
Leh
Rawalpindi
PAKISTAN
Dharmsala
TIBET
Dehradun
Delhi
Ganges
Nepal
Sikkim
Bhutan
Patan
Kathmandu
Bouda
Thimbu
Gangtok
Darjeeling
Lucknow
Gorakhpur
Jumna
Sarnath
Varanasi
Gaya
Bodh Gaya
Bangladesh
Dacca
Santiniketan
INDIA
Calcutta
Bombay
Hyderabad
ARABIAN SEA
BAY OF BENGAL
Madras
Bangalore
Mysore
SCALE OF MILES
0
100
200
300
Sri-Lanka
INDIAN OCEAN
Colombo

Map of India

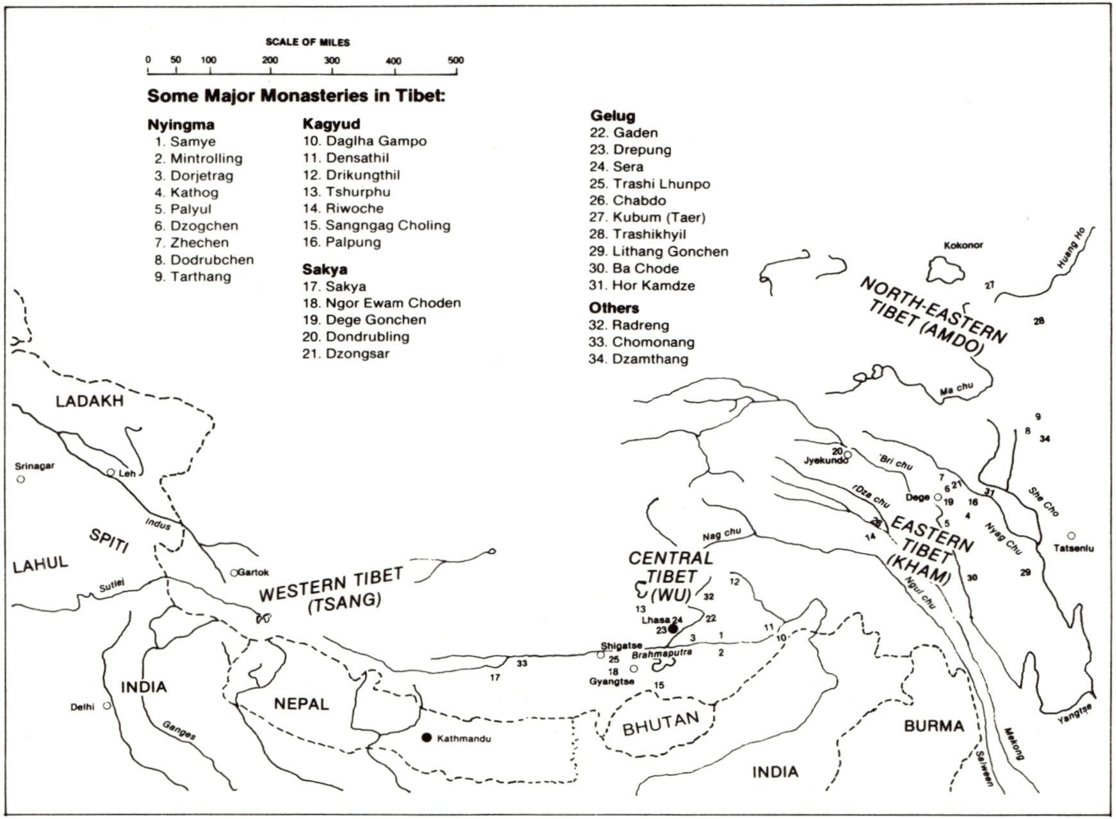
SCALE OF MILES
0 50 100 200 300 400 500
Some Major Monasteries in Tibet:
Nyingma
1. Samye
2. Mintrolling
3. Dorjetrag
4. Kathog
5. Palyul
6. Dzogchen
7. Zhechen
8. Dodrubchen
9. Tarthang
Kagyud
10. Daglha Gampo
11. Densathil
12. Drikungthil
13. Tshurphu
14. Riwoche
15. Sangngag Choling
16. Palpung
Sakya
17. Sakya
18. Ngor Ewam Choden
19. Dege Gonchen
20. Dondrubling
21. Dzongsar
Gelug
22. Gaden
23. Drepung
24. Sera
25. Trashi Lhunpo
26. Chabdo
27. Kubum (Taer)
28. Trashikhyil
29. Lithang Gonchen
30. Ba Chode
31. Hor Kamdze
Others
32. Radreng
33. Chomonang
34. Dzamthang
LADAKH
Srinagar
Leh
Indus
SPITI
LAHUL
Sutlej
Gartok
WESTERN TIBET
(TSANG)
INDIA
Delhi
Ganges
NEPAL
Kathmandu
CENTRAL
TIBET
(WU)
Nag chu
Lhasa
Shigatse
Brahmaputra
Gyangtse
BHUTAN
INDIA
BURMA
Salween
Mekong
Yangtse
EASTERN
TIBET
(KHAM)
Ngul chu
rDza chu
'Bri chu
Jyekundo
Dege
Nyag Chu
She Cho
Tatsenlu
NORTH-EASTERN
TIBET (AMDO)
Ma chu
Kokonor
Huang Ho

Map of Tibet showing some major monasteries

PART I

The Development of Buddhism in Tibet

INTRODUCTION

Twelve centuries after the Buddha's Mahāparinirvāṇa, Buddhism crossed the Himalayan ranges and reached Tibet, the Land of Snow, in the seventh century AD. In the following centuries Buddhism penetrated into all aspects of Tibetan life and culture and the Tibetan people found in the teaching of Lord Buddha a source of deep peace, happiness and fulfilment. Within the structure of a Buddhist teaching, various methods were developed which were suited to different types of individuals. These various methods are included within the three principal paths or yānas: Hinayāna, Mahāyāna and Vajrayāna. Tibetan Buddhism is unique in that it contains the scriptures, teachings and traditions of practice of all three yānas. Its almost infinite depth and richness make it one of the world's most profound living traditions. This essay is intended to give a brief account of its development.

When Buddhism reached Tibet, it encountered the ancient native religion called Bon, a type of shamanism in which the spirits of the sun, moon, mountains and trees are worshipped. The Bonpo, as they were called, also sacrificed animals as part of their religious practice. For several centuries Buddhism and Bon were in conflict with each other in Tibet. Buddhism emerged the victor but Bon has remained a living tradition until the present day. As a result of its encounter with Buddhism, Bon underwent deep and lasting changes. Many Bon texts were constructed on Buddhist models and as time passed the content of the Bon scriptures reflected Buddhist influence. Buddhist concepts were expressed in the terminology and language peculiar to the Bon texts. There were even a few great Tibetan Buddhist scholars who translated Buddhist texts into the Bon canon by using the vocabulary employed in the Bon writings. This was done with the aspiration that the numerous Bonpos of Tibet might also benefit from the Buddhist teachings.

Buddhism also had a profound effect on the political situation in Tibet. Part of the reason for its dramatic and almost total success within the country was because of the reverence and devotion of some of Tibet's greatest kings toward the teaching and principles of Buddhism. In giving an account of the development of Buddhism in Tibet we must consider the activities of these kings, because their support and patronage were crucial to the spread of Buddhism in Tibet.

Before the second century BC Tibet was not united. There were only small feudal principalities, warring factions and wandering nomads. Towards the end of the second century BC an exiled Indian prince reached Tibet and gained control over a substantial portion of the country. His Tibetan name was Nyathri Tsenpo and in 127 BC he was enthroned as the first king of Tibet. He built the first palace in the country, the Yumbu Lagang in Yarlung Valley. He and the lineage of kings that descended from him extended their control over the whole of Tibet. This lineage came to be known as the Chogyal (Chos rGyal, Dharma king) dynasty.

In AD 433 the 28th king of the Chogyal dynasty, Lhatho Thori Nyentsen (Lha Tho Tho Ri sNyan bTsan), received some Buddhist scriptures and religious objects. He did not understand the meaning of the scriptures but perceived that they and the sacred objects were things of great value and treated them with great reverence. This was the first appearance of Buddhist scriptures in Tibet.

The 33rd king of the Chogyal dynasty was Srongtsen Gampo (Srong bTsan sGam Po, 617–698) who was the first of the three great Dharma kings of Tibet. Before Srongtsen Gampo's time the Tibetan language had no written form. He sent his minister, Thonmi Sambhota, with many attendants to India in order to study the north Indian languages. After his return to Tibet, he developed the first Tibetan script on the basis of Indian models. He also wrote the basic grammar books for the Tibetan language and translated many Buddhist scriptures into Tibetan. Two of the wives of King Srongtsen Gampo also played an important part in the early history of Buddhism in Tibet. He married Princess Bhrikuti, daughter of King Amsuvarma of Nepal, and Princess Wen Ch'eng, daughter of the Emperor T'ang T'ai Tsung of China. Both of these women were devout Buddhists and they brought many priceless religious objects with them to Tibet. The most famous image of the Buddha in Tibet, the Jowo Yidzhin Norbu, was brought from China by the Princess Wen Ch'eng. They encouraged and supported the building of many Buddhist temples within the country. The Tsuglag Khang, the main temple of the capital city of Lhasa, was built under the patronage of King Srongtsen Gampo and Princess Bhrikuti. The king also constructed three codes of law for the people of the country based upon the principles and discipline of Buddhism. The reign of King Srongtsen Gampo marked the beginning of the practice of Buddhism in Tibet.

The 37th Chogyal, Thrisong Deutsen (Khri Srong De'u bTsan, AD 790–858), is the second of the three great kings of Tibet. He invited hundreds of Indian scholars and yogic masters to Tibet. The most famous were Sāntarakṣita, an abbot of Nalanda university, Guru Rinpoche or Padmasambhava, the greatest Indian tantric master, and Vimalamitra, a famous scholar and adept.

King Thrisong built the famous Samye monastery. Work was begun on the monastery in 810 and during his reign the first Tibetans took ordination as Bhikṣus (fully ordained monks). Working under the king's patronage, the great Indian scholars, along with 108 Tibetan translators, such as Vairocana and Kawa Paltseg, translated numerous sūtra and tantra texts from Sanskrit into Tibetan. During his reign Tibet attained a high degree of both secular power and spiritual development. Until the time of Langdarma, in the tenth century AD, his successors continued to extend and develop the doctrine of Dharma in Tibet.

The last of the three great dharma kings was Thri Ralpachen (Khri Ral Pa Can, 866–901), the 40th king of the Chogyal dynasty. His major contribution was to standardize the methods for translating Buddhist Sanskrit texts into Tibetan. All the texts translated up to this time were retranslated according to the new system. Henceforth, the translation of Buddhist texts was able to proceed with a high degree of accuracy and scholarly excellence. He also invited many great Indian scholars to Tibet and a great number of texts were translated into Tibetan. Unfortunately at the age of 36 he was murdered by his pro-Bon ministers.

King Thri Ralpachen's elder brother, Langdarma, became king in AD 901. He was the 41st and last king of the Chogyal dynasty. Langdarma was anti-Buddhist and with the help of his pro-Bon ministers he began the systematic destruction of Buddhism in central Tibet. The persecution fell especially heavily on the Bhikṣu Saṅgha. Many monks were forcibly disrobed or killed. The institutions of Buddhist monasticism disappeared from central Tibet for more than half a century. However, many Tantriks continued to practice covertly as laymen and the powerful tantric practitioner Nubchen Sangye Yeshe extracted a promise from the king not to harm the Tantriks or the tantric texts.

After five years of misrule Langdarma was killed by a Buddhist priest. After his death his sons fought among themselves for the vacant throne. However, no one of them was able to succeed and for three and a half centuries there was no effective central authority in the land. The different provinces assumed the position of independent states and were ruled by feudal lords.

During the time of Langdarma's persecution, three great monks fled to the province of Kham in eastern Tibet and maintained the tradition of the Vinaya ordination there. The greatest disciple of these three monks was Lachen Gongpa Rabsal (bLa Chen dGong Pa Rab gSal). After half a century of absence, the Vinaya lineage of Bhiksu ordination was brought from Kham back to central Tibet by ten students who had travelled from central Tibet to study with Lachen Gongpa Rabsal. By the middle of the tenth century AD the monasteries of central Tibet were able to resume their activities and the work of translation and practice was again carried forward.

The period we have been discussing so far down to the end of the tenth century is known in the Tibetan historical works as the period of the Early Spread of the Doctrine (bsTan Pa sNga Dar). The tantric texts that were translated up to the end of this period are known as the Earlier Translated Tantras (gSang sNgags sNga 'Gyur) or Old Tantras. Smṛtijñāna was the last great translator of this period. The lineage of teaching based on these texts is known as the Nyingma (the Old One). This remained a powerful Buddhist lineage in Tibet up until the present time, and will be discussed in some detail on the following pages.

The texts translated after the beginning of the eleventh century are known as the New Tantras (sNgags gSar Ma). Tibetan religious historians refer to this period of Tibetan history as the Later Spread (bsTan Pa Phyi Dar) of the Doctrine. The first great translator of the New Tantras was Rinchen Zangpo (Rin Chen bZang Po, 958-1051). Marpa Chokyi Lodro (Chos Kyi Blo Gros, 1012–1099) and Drogmi Sakya Yeshe ('Brog Mi Sakya Ye Shes, 993–1050) were also great translators of this period.

Various major and minor schools developed based on different texts within the New Tantras. The Kagyud school was founded by Marpa and the Sakya school was founded by Khon Konchong Gyalpo (dKon mChog rGyal Po, 1034-1102). The Kadam school was founded by the renowned Indian scholar of Vikramaśīla known as Atīśa (982–1054).

Before discussing the contributions of these various schools to the religious history of Tibet, it is necessary to conclude briefly our discussion of Tibetan political history. Increasingly during the period of the Later Spread of the Doctrine, especially after the development of the powerful Sakya and then Gelug schools in the fourteenth century, Buddhism exerted a powerful influence and then completely dominated the political life of Tibet.

This development began in the thirteenth century when Drogon Chogyal Phagpa ('Gro mGon Chos rGyal 'Phag Pa, 1235–1280) of the Sakya school became the spiritual tutor of Kublai Khan, the Mongolian king who eventually became the emperor of China. The Khan, in gratitude for Phagpa's teaching and blessing, made him the ruler of all Tibet in 1253. This was the first time that the supreme secular authority was held by a monk. After Phagpa, a series of Sakya rulers ruled Tibet for almost a hundred years.

In 1349 Changchub Gyaltshen (Byang Chub rGyal mTshan) of the Phagtru (Phag Gru) clan overthrew the Sakya rulers and became ruler of Tibet. Then a succession of eleven Phagtru rulers ruled Tibet for 106 years.

During this period, the celebrated scholar Lobzang Tragpa (Blo bZang Grags Pa, 1357–1419) from Tsongkha, Amdo in eastern Tibet founded the Gelug school. Tsongkhapa, as he was known, was a great scholar who wrote many works. He and his disciples built many large monasteries. He stressed the importance of the fundamental teachings of Buddhism and the strict observance of monastic discipline. In time the Gelug became one of the most politically powerful of the Tibetan Buddhist schools. From the seventeenth century until 1959 the Dalai Lamas of this school were both the spiritual and temporal leaders of Tibet.

Before the Gelug assumed power, Tibet was ruled by two successive feudal dynasties. In 1435 Donyod Dorje of the Rinpung clan overthrew the Phagtru king and four succeeding Rinpungpa kings ruled Tibet for 130 years. In 1566 Tsheten Dorje (Tshe brTan rDo rJe) of the Tsang pa (gTsang Pa) overthrew the Rinpung ruler and three succeeding kings of this dynasty ruled Tibet for seventy-six years.

Then in 1542 the forces of Gusri Khan of the Qosot Mongols defeated the Tsangpa rulers and offered the lordship of Tibet to the 5th Dalai Lama (1617–1682). The present Dalai Lama is the 14th in this lineage.

In Tibet the size and number of Buddhist monasteries as well as the number of monks and nuns reached its peak at the end of the 1950s when suddenly all ended in the gravest tragedy of Tibetan Buddhist history. Starting in 1959, Buddhism in Tibet has been totally destroyed at the hands of the Chinese communists. Since the late 1970s, as the political trends in China have changed, many of the religious institutions in Tibet are starting to be rebuilt from the ruins of the old ones and a limited number of monks and nuns are permitted to enrol. For example, according to reports Drepung monastery, which had 7,700 to 10,000 monks before 1959, now has an enrolment of about 600 monks, but we do not yet have any clear information on how many religious institutions have been rebuilt or how many monks or nuns are enrolled.

About 100,000 refugees from Tibet who are settled in exile, mainly in India, Nepal and Bhutan, are preserving and propagating as best they can the Buddhist and traditional culture.

In the following pages we will discuss briefly the various Buddhist schools which had developed in Tibet until 1959 and are now in exile.

1

THE NYINGMA (rNying Ma) SCHOOL
The Ancient One

THE EARLY SPREAD OF THE DOCTRINE

The Nyingma school was founded by the Indian tantric master, Padmasambhava, during the time of King Thrisong Deutsen in the ninth century AD. Various versions of his life are given in the Tibetan scriptures of the Nyingma tradition, of which the following is a general outline.

He was born from a lotus blossom in the Milk-Ocean in the country of Urgyan (Oḍḍiyāna) which modern scholars believe to be the Swat valley of Pakistan. He took birth eight years after the Buddha's Mahāparinirvāṇa. He attained the deathless Siddhi through tantric practice and at the age of more than 1000 years went to Tibet in the ninth century. His followers believe that he is still alive in the Rakasas' land (Srin Po'i Gling) and can be seen by realized persons.

After his lotus birth, King Indrabodhi of Oḍḍiyāna found him in the Milk-Ocean while he was returning from a successful trip in search of a Wishing-gem. The king brought him to his palace and as he had no heir, he made him the crown prince. Eventually Padmasambhava married Khadro Odchangma (mKha' 'Gro 'Od Chang Ma). But he asked the king to allow him to renounce the kingdom in order to lead a life of religious practice. When the king refused, Padmasambhava, exercising Skillful Means, killed the wicked minister's son—who was to die at that time because of his past karmic effects—while they were playing. According to the law of the land Padmasambhava was banished from the country to a cemetery where he took up tantric teachings and practices. This was in accordance with his wishes and he then visited other cemeteries to receive tantric teachings and perform tantric practices and he subdued the male and female spirits of those places. He was blessed by the Wisdom Ḍākinīs, Khadroma Zhiwatsho (mKha' 'Gro Ma Zhi Ba 'Tsho) and Vajra Vārāhī. He then visited different teachers and studied medicine, astrology, logic and art. He received Bhikṣu (monk) ordination from Ācārya Prabhāhasti. He studied the Yoga Śāstras from Ācārya Prabhāhasti, Vinaya from Ananda, and Tantra including Dzogpa Chenpo (rDzogs Pa Chen Po—Atiyoga, Skt.) from Prahevajra, Śrīsiṁha, Nāgārjuna, Hūṁkara, Vamalamitra and Buddhagūhya, who were all accomplished masters. Through his practice he received the attainments of the various tantras.

A very significant happening in his life occurred when he visited the Sahora kingdom. He gave teaching to the princess of the kingdom and her 500 ladies in waiting, all of whom were nuns. The news reached the king that a very handsome stranger—like the son of the gods—was staying with the princess and her maidens. The king ordered that the Guru be burnt in a mountain valley filled with wood and oil. The Guru was wrapped in many cloths and burned before the people of Sahora. After a few days the Guru was not only unharmed but with his miraculous powers he had transformed the burning oil and wood into a mountain lake. He was sitting on a lotus blossom in the middle of the lake attended by many gods and ḍākinīs.

Upon seeing this the king and his subjects repented of their evil ways and Padmasambhava was taken to the king's palace as a guest of honor. The king himself received teachings from him and offered him his kingdom and the hand of the Princess Mandāravā. The Guru took Mandāravā as his consort and together they went to the Maratika cave, located in what is now Nepal, in order to do tantric practice. There they both achieved the Deathless Attainment.

Then Padmasambhava with his consort decided to return to the kingdom of Oḍḍiyāna. Upon arriving in the country he was recognized by the evil minister whose son he had killed and the king ordered that he and his consort be burnt in a big fire of sandalwood. After a few days the Guru by his miraculous power had transformed the fire into a beautiful lake and he and his consort were sitting on a lotus blossom in the middle of the lake. The king, ministers and all the people had faith in him as a great teacher and he remained in Oḍḍiyāna for thirteen years as the chaplain of the palace. He gave powerful tantric teachings such as the Kadu Choki Gyatsho (bKa' 'Dus Chos Kyi rGya mTsho), a condensed text of sādhanas, and many fortunate people of the land including the king attained the Vidyādhara siddhi. After leaving Oḍḍiyāna the Guru went to Nepal in order to do further practice. With the support of the Nepalese princess Śākya Devi he achieved the Supreme

Attainment through the deep practice of the sādhanas of Yangdag and Dorje Phurba (rDo dJe Phur Ba-Vajrakīla) divinities. Through this practice he attained and has remained in the form (body) of Mahāmudrā Vidyādhara.

He then visited many parts of India such as Hurmuja (a small island of Oḍḍiyāna), Sikodhara, Dhanakosa, Rukma, Tirahuti, Kamaru, Tharu, Champa, Khasya, Trilinga (South India), Kañci and Maghadha (Central India). In these places he manifested different forms and subdued the evil spirits wherever he went. He gave various kinds of teachings and many of his disciples attained siddhis (attainments) which result from the successful practice of meditation and yoga.

At this time the great Dharma King Thrisong Deutsen (790–858) was ruling Tibet. He was the most powerful ruler in Tibetan history and under his guidance Tibetan forces captured Ch'ang-An, the capital of the Tang dynasty, and also penetrated all the way to Maghadha in central India. King Trisong Deutsen, as well as being a powerful secular ruler, was also deeply devoted to the cause of Buddhism. He invited the great Indian Buddhist scholar and saint Śāntarakṣita, an abbot of Nalanda university, to Tibet. The king and the abbot launched the building of Samye monastery, the first Buddhist monastery in the country. However, because of the influence of the king's wicked ministers and the local evil spirits, it was impossible to carry out the building of the monastery. At the suggestion of Śāntarakṣita the king invited Padmasambhava, who by this time had the reputation of being the most powerful tantric master in India, to Tibet in order to defeat the forces obstructing the construction of the monastery. It was for this reason that Padmasambhava travelled to Tibet. He quickly pacified and subdued all the forces opposed to the construction of Samye monastery, as well as defeating all the other forces that were attempting to prevent the teaching of the Dharma in the Land of Snows. He gave both Mahāyāna and Tantrayāna teachings to many fortunate persons. Together with his realized consort, Khadro Yeshe Tshogyal (mKh' 'Gro Ye Shes mTsho rGyal), he travelled with his miraculous power throughout Tibet doing various tantric practices, performing miracles, giving teachings and blessing hundreds of caves, mountains, lakes, monasteries and temples as sacred places. Hundreds of Tibetans who received his teaching and blessing attained siddhis. He had twenty-five principal disciples (rJe 'Bang Nyer lNga) including the king.

The great Samye, with its main temple, twelve smaller temples, four great stupas and 108 smaller stupas all surrounded by a high wall, was completed within five years. It was the center from which Buddhism spread to all corners of Tibet. Many great Indian pandits were invited to Tibet by the king and they worked with Tibetan scholars on the translation of the Buddhist scriptures from Sanskrit into Tibetan. In one of the smaller temples (sGra bsGyur rGya Gar Gling) of Samye monastery, 100 Indian pandits and Tibetan translators worked together on the translations of sūtras and tantras. Many Tibetan texts were also brought from other lands by the miraculous power of Guru Rinpoche (as Padmasambhava is called by the Tibetans) and were translated into Tibetan. Thus when the great Indian Buddhist scholar Atīśa, who visited Tibet in AD 1042, saw the library at Samye monastery, he was surprised to find so many tantras which he had never seen in India. 'These tantras,' he said, 'may have been brought from the Land of Ḍākinīs by the power of Guru Rinpoche.' In the biography of Atīśa it is said that that was one of the three reasons why he realized that there is no end of tantras.

Thus the mission of Guru Rinpoche to Tibet firmly established Buddhism in the Snow Land. He cleared away the forces that were hindering it and taught the dharma in such a skilful manner that many Tibetans attained realization. The school that grew out of his mission is known as the Nyingma and it has survived through an unbroken lineage of masters until the present day.

But Padmasambhava's work in Tibet did not end with the establishment of Buddhism. He told the king that by his meditative power he could transform Tibet into a rich and prosperous land. He transformed barren, rocky lands into pastures and caused water to spring from rocks. Unfortunately some of the king's ministers were anti-Buddhist and they told the king that the Indian Tantrik was turning Tibet into a developed land in order to make it a part of India. The ministers intrigued against him and forced the king to ask him to return to India. The king prostrated before the Guru, made offerings of gold, and with a heavy heart asked him to return to India. Padmasambhava said that he had not come to Tibet for gold. He told the king that for him everything was gold and to prove his point he transformed several ordinary objects into gold. Then he said:

> "The mind of the king was changed by the ministers,
> The ministers and evil spirits of Tibet are mischievous.
> For sentient beings who are experiencing the result of bad karma,
> Even the Victorious Ones (Buddhas) are powerless to help them."

Before leaving for India the Guru gave the teaching of the Men Ngag Tawa'i Threngwa (Man Ngag lTa Ba'i 'Phreng Ba) to the king and others. When he left, a large party accompanied him part of the way to see him off. The wicked ministers sent eighteen men to kill him but when they encountered Padmasambhava, he made them motionless by his miraculous power.

There is some dispute among Tibetan scholars about the length of the Guru's stay in Tibet. Some accounts say that he was forced to leave Tibet because of the influence of the anti-Buddhist ministers. But the Nyingma accounts of his mission in Tibet say that only one of his magical emanations left the country and the real Guru remained in Tibet at the request of the king. These accounts state that the Guru remained for fifty-five years six months. During this time he visited many solitary places with his consort Yeshe Tshogyal and continued to perform powerful tantric practices in the country. Some accounts say that he visited Samye monastery and gave teachings there and again was threatened by the king's ministers. This time these ministers were finally silenced by a display of his tantric powers. The accounts that support Padmasambhava's long stay in Tibet (fifty-five years six months) agree that he only left Tibet during the reign of King Thrisong Deutsen's son, Prince Muthri Tsenpo. He finally left for the Rākṣasas' land in the year 864 with an impressive display of his magical power by riding a horse through the air at a place called Gungthang Lathog before the king, Muthri Tsenpo, his ministers and thousands of people who had gathered to see him off.

Guru Rinpoche visited many places in Tibet, snow peaks, caves, forests, lakes, and temples. He blessed these places and in some of them he concealed various materials, including dharma texts recording teachings in full or symbolic form, prophesies of the future of Tibet, and sacred objects and images. The teachings he entrusted to his disciples and the concealed objects and symbolic scripts to the protection of Dharmapālas, who would hand them over at the appointed times in future ages to the appropriate Tertons (gTer sTon-Dharma treasure revealers).

Before considering the teachings of the Nyingma school, we must first round out our account of the activities of King Thrisong Deutsen and his immediate successors who contributed to the establishment of Buddhism in Tibet. King Thrisong Deutsen invited many other great Indian scholars and saints to Tibet along with Padmasambhava and Śāntaraṣita. Mahapandita Vimalamitra, Dharmakīrti, Buddhagupta, Kamalaśīla, Visuddhasiddha, Śāntagararbha and Mañjuśrī came to Tibet from India, Kashmir and Nepal. Also the Tibetan scholars and translators Vairocana, Kawa Paltseg, Chogro Lu'i Gyaltsen and Zhang Yeshe De went to India and Nepal many times to receive Buddhist teaching and bring back texts to Tibet. During this time hundreds of texts were translated into Tibetan including texts from the Vinaya, Abhidharma, Hibayāna and Mahāyāna sūtras as well as tantric texts. These special tantras of the Nyingma school—Mahāyoga, Anuyoga and Atiyoga (rDzogs Pa Chen Po)—were translated into Tibetan by Padmasambhava, Vimalamitra and Vairocana during this time.

It was during this era that the first Tibetans took monastic ordination. The king wanted to determine whether or not Tibetans were capable of upholding the many (254) and strict vows which fully ordained Bhikṣus must maintain. Seven men were selected for a test case and these men are known in Tibetan historical records as the Seven Men of Trial (Sad Mi Mi bDun). They were successful in keeping the vows and hundreds of Tibetans followed in their footsteps and became fully ordained monks. Two saṅghas (religious communities) were founded: the Saṅgha of Renounced Ones (Bhikṣus) and the Saṅgha of Tantriks.

The succession of kings who followed Thrison Deutsen until the time of Langdarma supported and encouraged the spread of Dharma. This period of Tibetan religious history culminated in the reign of King Ralpachen (866–901). He invited the Indian scholars Jinamitra, Śīlendrabodhi, Surendrabodhi and Dānaśīla to Tibet and together with the Tibetan translators they carried on the work of translating the Buddhist scriptures. At this time the Tibetan grammatical systems were revised and strict rules were laid down in order to ensure the accuracy of the translations. These rules were known as the Gyalpo'i Kachad, the rules by the order of the king. Unfortunately the king was killed by anti-Buddhist ministers at the age of 36 and his older brother, Langdarma, who was actively against the Dharma, came to power and severely persecuted Buddhism in Central Tibet. He ruled only five years before being killed by a Buddhist priest, but his suppression of Buddhism was so thorough that the exoteric aspect of the Dharma disappeared from Central Tibet for half a century. This ends the period known as the Early Spread of the Doctrine in which the Nyingma lineage was firmly established in the Land of Snow.

THE TRANSMISSION OF THE NYINGMA TEACHINGS

The transmission or way in which the teachings of a spiritual lineage originate, particularly if the teachings have mystical and yogic aspects and are handed down from one generation to the next, is very important. It is necessary that the accuracy of the teachings be maintained if they are to be efficacious. Thus all effective spiritual traditions pay great attention to the transmissions of their teachings and take great pains to ensure that they are properly communicated from generation to generation. We will now consider the manner in which the profound body of Nyingma teachings was transmitted to the generations of practitioners.

Many sūtra teachings of the Buddha and of Buddhist scholars, which were translated in the period of the earlier translation, are still present and being practiced in their respective lineages. The vinaya teachings and the lineage of bhikṣu ordination survived by bringing back the earlier tradition from Kham to central Tibet. Most Tibetan bhikṣus today belong to this tradition from the Earlier Spread. The complete scriptures of the original Abhidharma from the Tripiṭaka never reached Tibet. The Abhidharma of Asaṅga and Vasubandhu were translated during the Earlier Spread by Jinamitra and the translator Kawa Paltseg. They taught the Abhidharma to Lhalung Paldor and We (dBas) Yeshes Gyalwa. The latter went to Kham where he spread these teachings.

Prajñāpāramitā texts were translated and taught by Lang Khampa Gocha. Madhyamaka texts were translated and taught by Paṇḍita Jñānagarbha, the translator Chogro Lu'i Gyaltshen, Śāntarakṣita, Kamalaśīla, and others.

With the translators Kawa Paltseg, Chogro Lu'i Gyaltshen and Nanam Yeshe Gyaltshen, Ācāryas Dānaśīla and Kamalaśīla translated the following sūtras: Kontseg (dKon brTsegs-Ratnakūṭa), Phalwoche (Phal Bo Che-Avataṁsaka), Sherchin (Sher Phyin-Prajñāpāramitā). The Chinese Ācārya Kamalaśīla with the translator Ma Rinchen Chog (rMa Rin Chen mChog) translated many sūtras from the Chinese. Along with the Tibetan translators Śāntarakṣita translated many texts of the Tripiṭaka. Padmasambhava with Nub Nankha'i Nyingpo (sNubs Nam mKha'i sNying Po) and others translated many tantras. With the translator Nyag (gNyags) Jñānakumara, Ācārya Vimalamitra translated many inner and outer tantras. The names of the translators are recorded at the end of each text in both the Kagyur and the Tengyur.

The Nyingma system of teaching has six levels of tantras: the three outer tantras and the three inner tantras. The three outer tantras are the Kriyātantra, Caryātantra and Yogatantra. The uniquely Nyingma scriptures are the three inner tantras: Mahāyoga, Anuyoga and Atiyoga. The three outer tantras were brought to Tibet by Ācārya Buddhagupta and others. The three inner tantras reached Tibet as follows:

(1) **Mahāyoga:** Vajrasattva taught the eighteen great tantras to King Ja of Sahora in India. This king also received them from Vimalakīrti who had received them from Vajrapāṇi at the Malaya mountain (Śrīpāda) in Śrī Lankā. After they had passed through many teachers Buddhagūhya received them and then transmitted them to Vimalamitra. He gave the teachings of Mahāyoga to the Tibetan translators Ma (rMa), Nyag (gNyag) and others. Padmasambhava also taught some of these tantras to his disciples, including the Drubpa Kagyed (sGrub Pa bKa' brGyad), the Eight Sadhanas of Great Maṇḍalas.

(2) **Anuyoga:** King Ja also received the teachings of this yana from Vajrasattva and Vimalakīrti. The king then taught them to siddha Kukuripa and they passed through many teachers, finally reaching the Tibetan Nubchen Sangye Yeshe (gNub Chen Sangs rGyas Ye Shes), who was one of the twenty-five principal disciples of Padmasambhava. He taught them in Tibet and his lineage has survived to the present day.

(3) **Atiyoga:** Vajrasattva transmitted these teachings to the Nirmāṇakāya emanation Garab Dorje (dGa Rab rDo rJe-Prahevajra) who passed them to a lineage of teachers including Padmasambhava, Vimalamitra and Vairocana who taught them to Tibetans. Atiyoga (rDzogs Pa Chen Po) has three divisions: Semde (Sems sDe-Cittavarga), Longde (Klong sDe-Ābhyantarvarga) and Men-ngagde (Man Ngag sDe-Upadeśavarga). The first two divisions of the Atiyoga teachings were brought to Tibet by Vairocana, Tibet's greatest translator. The Man-ngagde which is also known as the Man-ngag Nyingthig (Man Ngag sNying Thig—Instructions on the Innermost Essence of the Heart) are the deepest teachings of the Nyingma school. They were brought to Tibet by Padmasambhava and Vimalamitra and then passed through two lineages of transmission. The first was taught by Vimalamitra and passed through various teachers until it reached the great Nyingma saint and scholar Kunkhyen Longchen Rabjam (Kun mKhyen kLong Chen Rab 'Byams, 1308–1363). The second lineage of transmission was taught by Padmasambhava to his consort Khadro Yeshe Tshogyal (mKha' 'Gro Ye Shes mTso rGyal) and Princess Pema Sal (Padma gSal). He concealed these teachings to be rediscovered at a later time. A few centuries later a reincarnation of the Princess Pema Sal called Pema Lethro Tsal (Padma Las 'Phro rTsal) discovered the texts and her

incarnation Kunkhyen Longchan Rabjam composed extraordinary commentaries on them. Thus in the figure of Kunkhyen Longchen Rabjam the two Nyingthig lineages converged. He was the greatest scholar and saint of the middle period of the Nyingma tradition. He wrote 200 treatises on various subjects and his writings are some of the most important treasures of the Nyingma lineage and especially of the Man-ngag Nyingthig transmission. In the later period of the Nyingma school, the most important propagator of the teachings was Kunkhyen Jigmed Lingpa (Kun mKhyen 'Jigs Med Gling Pa, 1729-1798), who was a great teacher and writer.

The teachings of the Nyingma tantras are transmitted through two major systems: Ringgyud Kama (Ring brGyud bKa' Ma—the Long Transmission of the Canon) and Nyegyud (Nye brGyud gTer Ma—the Short Transmission through the Discovered Dharma Treasures). The Kama teachings were transmitted by earlier teachers to their disciples through an unbroken lineage of teachers and students. The Termas are the teachings concealed by Guru Rinpoche to be discovered in later times by highly realized lamas, the rebirths of his disciples, known as Tertons (gTer sTon—Dharma Treasure Discoverers).

1 Long transmission of the Canon

These are the tantric teachings which the Buddha himself taught through the manifestation of various divinities. Most of them were taught by the Primordial Buddha Dharmakāya (Samantabhadra) and transmitted to disciples in various ways. According to the Nyingma school the transmission of tantric teaching occurs in three stages:

(1) The Primordial Buddha transmits the teaching to his inseparable disciples, the Saṃbhogakāya Buddhas, through direct Mind Transmission (dGongs brGyud) without verbal or physical symbols.

(2) The Saṃbhogakāya Buddhas such as Vajrasattva transmit teaching to Nirmāṇakāya emanations in different realms including the human realm through Indication Transmission (brDa brGyud). This type of transmission is accomplished by verbal and physical indications.

(3) In India and Tibet most teachers transmit teaching to their disciples through Hearing Transmission (sNyan brGyud). This method is the most commonly used for ordinary beings. Beginning with Padmasambhava, Vimalamitra and other teachers, the Hearing Transmission was started in Tibet and it has continued until the present day. The Mind Transmission and Indication Transmission also still exist

among teachers of high tantric meditational attainment. All of these systems of transmission are very important because according to the tantric teaching it is necessary to receive the proper transmission in order to practice. Tantric meditation practiced without receiving the proper transmission is dangerous or unbeneficial.

2 Short transmission of Discovered Dharma Treasures

The Terma transmission is referred to as a short transmission because the lineages connected with it are generally very short. For example, if a disciple of Padmasambhava takes rebirth as a Terton in the twentieth century, there is no need to have a long lineage of lamas preceding him. He himself has received the blessing and empowerment from Padmasambhava, attained realization, and is thus second to Padmasambhava in the lineage of transmission.

At the time of Padmasambhava's mission in Tibet he and his consort Yeshe Tshogyal transmitted and concealed many teachings and religious objects to be discovered by future disciples. The disciples who discovered them were known as Tertons. These lamas discovered the teachings and objects through their high attainments in meditation and communicated them to disciples who were ready to hear them. Padmasambhava himself foretold the people who would become Tertons and gave details of their births.

The first Terton, Sangye Lama (Sangs rGyas Bla Ma) appeared in the eleventh century. Following him, there were hundreds of lamas who specialized in the discovery of these treasures. There were 100 great Tertons and 1000 minor ones. Among the 100 Tertons there were five great ones who were known as the Five Kings. They were: (1) Nyangral Nyima Odzer (Nyang Ral Nyi Ma 'Od Zer, 1124–1192); (2) Guru Chowang (Chos dBang, 1212–1270); Dorje Lingpa (rDo rJe Gling Pa, 1346–1405); (4) Padma Lingpa (1450–?); and (5) Jamyang Khyentse ('Jam dByangs mKhyen brTse, 1820–1892).

THE NYINGMA SCRIPTURES

Most of the important Sūtra, Adhidharma, Vinaya, Prajñapāramitā and Tantric texts are contained in the Kagyur or Kajur (bKa' 'Gyur) collection of the Buddha's canon which contains 1046 treatises in 104 volumes. The Nyingmapas also study the works contained in the Tengyur or Tenjur (bsTan 'Gyur) collection, which consists of commentaries by Indian Buddhist scholars on the sūtras and tantras. This collection contains 3863 treatises in 221 volumes.

There is also a large body of literature important to the Nyingma school which is not included in these two large collections. Some of the most important texts are given as follows: (1) the Nyingma Gyudbum (rNying Ma rGyud 'Bum) which is a collection of ancient tantras in thirty-three volumes which was recently reprinted in New Delhi; (2) the Terma literature of the 100 Great Tertons. One of the most important collections of this literature is the Rinchen Terdzod (Rin Chen gTer mDzod) in sixty volumes compiled by Kongtrul Yonten Gyatsho (Kong sPrul Yon Tan rGya mTsho, 1913–1899). This collection was published under the auspices of Venerable Khyentse Rinpoche (who presently lives in Bhutan); (3) the Men-ngag Tathreng (ManNgag lTa 'Phreng) and Mamo Sangwa Le Kyi Thigle (Ma Mo gSang Ba Las Kyi Thig Le) by Guru Padmasambhava; and (4) the works of Vimalamitra and Vairocana.

Some of the most important scholarly works by Nyingma saints and scholars are listed as follows: (1) the works of Rongzom Chokyi Zangpo (Rong Zom Chos Kyi bZang Po, tenth century); (2) the 200 treatises of Kunkhyen Longchen Rabjam (1308–1363); (3) the works of Paltrul (dPal sPrul Rin Po Che, 1808–?); (4) the works of Mipham Rinpoche (1846–1912) in thirty-two volumes; (5) the works of the 3rd Dodrub Chen Rinpoche (rDo Grub Chen Rin Po Che, 1865–1926) in six volumes; and (6) the works of Khenpo Zhenga (mKhan Po gZhan dGa', 1871–1927) in fifteen volumes.

NYINGMA DOCTRINE

The Nyingma school classifies all of the Buddha's teachings and paths to enlightenment into Nine Yānas. The first three yānas are called the Hetulakṣaṇayānas or Yānas of Cause. They are known as the Śrāvakayāna, Pratyekabuddhayāna and the Bodhisattvayāna. The last six yānas are called the six Phalayānas or Yānas of Result. These yānas contain the tantric teachings and are known as the Three Outer Tantras and Three Inner Tantras. We will now give a brief explanation of each of these yanas.

(1) Śrāvakayāna (Vehicle of Listeners; Hinayāna). The disciples of

this yāna accept any one of the eight pratimoksa vows of moral discipline. They accept the selflessness of persons (Pudgala nairātmya) but not the selflessness of phenomena (Dharma nairātmya). The mind and body are relaxed through the practice of tranquillity meditation. They do insight meditation on the Four Truths and their sixteen aspects and through the perfection of the four paths—Sambhāramārga, Prayogamārga, Darśanamārga and Bhāvanāmārga—they attain peace and happiness for themselves. They attain gradually the four stages of result: Stream Enterer, Once Returner, Never Returner, and Arhat.

(2) Pratyekabuddhayāna (Silent Buddha; Hinayāna). The disciples of this path observe any one of the eight pratimoksa vows as do the Śrāvakas. They assert the view of Pudgala nairātmya, but in regard to the view of Dharma nairātmya, they accept the selflessness of objects but they hold the view that the smallest moment of consciousness is true. They practice tranquillity meditation, meditation on the Four Truths with their sixteen aspects of interdependent arising (Pratītyasamutpāda). Through these efforts one can attain the state of Arhathood for oneself.

(3) Bodhisattvayāna (Mahāyāna). The disciples of this path assert that all persons and phenomena are without any self or truth. They practice many of the same meditations as in the above two yānas but practice is done with the intention of achieving enlightenment or Buddhahood for the benefit of all living beings. This intention to achieve enlightenment for the benefit of all is known as 'Bodhicitta' and is one of the distinctive marks of the Mahāyāna path. In addition, they practice the Six Perfections (pāramitās): generosity (dāna), ethnics (śīla), patience (kṣānti), strenuousness (vīrya), contemplation (samādhi) and wisdom (prajñā). They train in the Four Paths, meditate on the twofold no-self (Nairātmya) and the thirty-seven Wings of Enlightenment (Bodhipākṣi). After practicing for three countless eons (asaṅkhyakalpa) they attain the Mahāparinirvāṇa, Supreme Enlightenment. After attaining this state they continue to appear in the world of beings in various forms until all creatures attain enlightenment.

The next six yānas of the Nyingma are all within the practice of the path of Tantra. An ancient tantra, Tshul gSum sGron Me, gives a brief indication of the meaning of the Tantric path:

> The aim is the same, but there is no delusion,
> There are many skillful means and no difficulties,
> It is for people of sharp intellect,
> Hence, the Tantrayāna is supreme.

The goal of all the yānas is the same—enlightenment or Buddhahood—but the way of practice is different. In the lower yānas, one attempts to avoid defilement or uses various means as antidotes against defilement. But on the tantric paths the defilements themselves are used as a means to attainment. The goal is to see all aspects of existence as perfect and pure. This is the skillful means to attain Buddhahood.

The Three Outer Tantras (Phyi rGyud sDe gSum)

(1) Kriyāyoga (Bya rGyud). Disciples of this path concentrate on the purification of body, speech and mind. They live mostly on vegetarian foods, sweets and dairy products. They assert that within Absolute Truth (Parmārthasatya) all things are equal, but in the Relative Truth (Saṁvṛitisatya) they hold that the divinities are lords and the disciples are servants. They visualize the divinity in front of them and make offerings and recite prayers and mantras. Generally, the devotee does not visualize himself as the divinity. By meditating on the body, speech and mind of the divinity the disciple receives the divinity's blessing. After sixteen lifetimes of such practice one will attain the Trikula Vajradhara state.

(2) Caryāyoga (sPyod rGyud). The disciples of this path maintain the same philosophical view as in the Yogatantra (below) and practice much as in the Kriyāyoga tantra (above). The main difference is that they visualize the divinity as a friend or close relation and concentrate on the stabilization of their contemplation. They attain the state of Vajradhara within seven lives.

(3) Yogatantra (rNal 'Byor rGyud). The disciples of this path maintain that within Absolute Truth all existents are free from any conceptualization, are empty and shine with radiant clarity. Within Relative Truth all appearances are regarded as the maṇḍalas of divinities. They do not pay much attention to the cleaning of the body, speech or mind as these things are automatically purified as a result of meditation. Their meditation has two aspects: with characteristics and without characteristics. In the first stage the disciples visualize themselves as the divinity and then invite the wisdom divinity (Ye shes Pa) and dissolve it into the visualized form (Dam Tshing Pa). Then offerings etc. are made. In the second stage, the disciples concentrate on the meaning of Tathatā, the non-duality of characteristicless absolute nature and all appearances, which are divinities.

The Three Inner Tantras (Nang rGyud sDe gSum)

In the outer tantras the distinction between the Two Truths is maintained, divinities are not visualized with their female consorts, the five meats are not taken and one does not attain the final result in this lifetime. In the inner tantras the Two Truths are held to be inseparable, all phenomena are equal, the five meats and five nectars are taken, the divinities are visualized with their consorts, and the final result can be attained in this life. The tantras of these three yānas are the special and distinctive Nyingma practices.

(1) Mahāyoga. The disciples of this path enjoy all things without being in any way attached to them. Within absolute truth all things are accepted as the essence of the mind and the Dharmakāya. All manifestation, thoughts and appearance are considered to be the sacred aspects of the divinites within relative truth. The disciple purifies all existents as divinities and concentrates on the non-duality of bliss, clarity and no-thought. One can attain enlightenment in this life.

(2) Anuyoga. This practice does not concentrate so much on the visualization of the deities. Rather, the disciple stresses the perfection (rDzogs Rim) of bliss, clarity and no-thought (bDe Ba, gSal Ba and Mi rTog Pa). This is done through yogic practices on the veins, semen and energy (rTsa, Thig Le and rLung) in the body. They assert that all appearances are the three great maṇḍalas which are Spontaneous, Empty and Great Bliss. There are two paths contained within the tantra: the Path of Liberation (Grol Lam) and the Path of Skillful Means (Thabs Lam). In the path of liberation one meditates on the no-thought wisdom and sees all appearances as divinities and their Pure Land. In the path of skillful means one attains wisdom by using the four or six cakras of the body. Through these practices one may attain Buddhahood in this life.

(3) Atiyoga (rDzogs Pa Chen Po-Mahāsandhiyoga, Skt.). This is the highest teaching of the Nyingma, and it is exclusively a Nyingma teaching and practice.

Dzogchen practitioners assert that all the appearances or apparent phenomena are illusions of the deluded mind. They are false because in reality their nature is free from conceptualizations. In nature all existents are the same and they are pure in the Dharmakāya. In practice there is no acceptance or rejection, rather all existents are accepted as manifestations of the nature, Dharmatā.

There are three aspects in Dzogchen teachings: Semde (sems sDe-

Cittavarga), Longde (kLong sDe-Abhyantarvarga) and Men-ngagde (Man Ngag sDe-Upadeśavarga). These teachings are instructions which introduce the student to the nature of the mind or the nature of all existents, the Dharmatā (ultimate nature), by the innermost direct method of practice. After receiving the introduction to this nature, one maintains the practice to make clear and to stabilize this state of Awareness and to attain freedom from worldly defilements forever. When this meditation on the nature of mind is perfected, all existents will dissolve into the vast expanse of Dharmatā, the Dharmakāya.

IMPORTANT NYINGMA MONASTERIES AND INSTITUTIONS

There are about 1000 Nyingma monasteries and temples in Tibet. Some of the major ones are as follows:

The Samye monastery built by Guru Padmasambhava and Śāntarakṣita in the ninth century is the most important as it was Tibet's first major monastic institution. Lately, this monastery has been under the jurisdiction of followers of the Sakya school. The Tsuglag Khang (gTsug Lag Khang) and Ramoche temples of Lhasa built by King Srongstsen Gampo in the seventh century and many other ancient temples are of Nyingma origin. However, in recent centuries most of these temples are now administered by the Gelug order.

Some of the important monasteries of the present day are given as follows:

In central Tibet: Mintroling (sMin Grol Gling) monastery built by Terchen Gyurmed Dorje (gTer Chen 'Gyur Med rDo rJe, 1646-1714) in 1676; Dorje Trag (rDo rJe Brag) monastery built by Rigdzin Ngagi Wangpo (Rig 'Dzin Ngag Gi dBang Po) in 1659.

In Kham province: Kathog monastery built by Kadampa Desheg (bDe gShegs, 1122–1192) in 1159; Palyul (dPal Yul) monastery built by Rigdzin Kunsang Sherab (Rig 'Dzin Kun bZang Shes Rab) in 1665; Dzogchen (rDzogs Chen) monastery built by Padma Rigdzin (1625–1697) in 1685; Zhechen monastery built by the 2nd Rabjam Gyurmed Kunzang Namgyal (Rab 'Byam 'Gyur Med bZang rNamrGyal) in 1735; Khordong ('Khor bDong) monastery of the Chang Ter (byang gTer) tradition; Tungkar monastery of Sertha.

In Golok and Amdo provinces: the Dodrub Chen (mDo Grub Chen) monastery built by the 2nd Dodrub Chen Rinpoche; Tarthang monastery built by Lhatul Rinpoche; Rongwo Sribgon and Rongwo Nyingon of Rekong.

There are also a large number of Nyingma monasteries in Bhutan and some in Sikkim, Ladakh and parts of Nepal. In recent years there are also a growing number of Nyingma centers and temples in Europe and the United States.

In general the Nyingma tradition in Tibet did not have one head for the whole school. But since coming to India, the Nyingmapas recognized Dudjom Rinpoche, the incarnation of the great Terton Dudjom Lingpa, as supreme head with his main seat in Nepal. Dudjom Rimpoche passed away on January 17, 1987.

Tibetan Buddhist schools which resulted from the Later Spread of the Doctrine

The persecution of the Dharma by the anti-Buddhist King Langdarma marks the end of the Earlier Spread of the Doctrine in central Tibet. Towards the end of the tenth century Buddhism began to reappear in central Tibet. The eleventh century in Tibetan religious history was a time of great progress and development of Buddhism. Many new teachers and texts arrived from India during this period and many Tibetans went to India to study. The tantric texts which were translated during the eleventh century and afterwards are known as the New Tantras. These texts, and teachers who had mastered the teachings, founded new Buddhist schools in Tibet. These schools are generally known as the Sarma or New Ones. We begin our survey of these schools with the Kagyud school.

2

THE KAGYUD (bKa' brGyud) SCHOOL

Transmission of the oral teaching

The Kagyud school has two main schools and many minor ones. The two main schools are: Shangpa Kagyud (Shangs Pa bKa' brGyud) and Dagpo Kagyud (Dvags Po bKa' brGyud).

A Shangpa Kagyud

This school was established by the great yogi and siddha Khyungpo Naljor (rNal 'Byor—the yogi of Khyungpo, 978–1079). He spent fifty years studying sūtra and tantra in India, Nepal and Tibet. He had many teachers including Sukhasiddha, Rāhulagupta and the rainbow body form of Niguma, the consort of Mahāsiddha Nāropa. The Zhang Zhong monastery in Shang valley was his principal monastery. In addition, he built 100 other monasteries. He taught for thirty years and had 80,000 disciples.

His main teachings were on the five tantras: Cakrasaṁvara, Hevajra, Mahāmāyā, Guhyasamāja and Vajrabhairava. He also transmitted the teachings of Niguma, Sukhasiddha and the doctrine of Mahāmudrā. There is no longer a separate school of this tradition, but the teachings are being practiced by many Kagyud Lamas.

B Dagpo Kagyud

'Dagpo Kagyud' translated literally means transmission of the order (canon) of Dagpo (Dvags po). Dagpo is one of the names for the great scholar and yogi Gampopa who lived in the Dagpo valley and played a decisive role in the establishment of this school in Tibet.

The founder of the school was Marpa Lotsawa (also known as Chos Kyi Blo Gros, 1012–1099). He first studied with Drogmi Lotsawa ('Brog Mi Lo Tsa Ba, 993–1050) in Tibet and he then went to India three times and Nepal four times. He took teachings from 108 teachers. His two principal teachers were the Indian Mahāsiddhas Maitrīpa and Nāropa, both of whom were among the eighty-four Mahāsiddhas of Buddhist India. He learned many tantric teachings including the doctrine of Mahāmudrā from these realized teachers. Through the teaching and blessing of Mahāsiddha Maitrīpa he accomplished the absolute realization of Mahāmudrā. Upon returning to Tibet he transmitted the teachings of Cakrasaṁvara, Guhyasamāja, Hevajra, Mahāmāyā and other tantras to his disciples. His four principal disciples were known as the Four Pillars. They were: Ngogton Choku Dorje (rNgog sTon Chos sKu rDo rJe), Tshurton Wangngo (mTshur sTong dBang Ngo), Meton Tsonpo (Mes sTon Tshon Po) and Milarepa (Mi La Ras Pa).

Milarepa (1040–1123) was Marpa's greatest disciple and much of the teaching of this school passed through him. He was one of the most famous yogis and poets in Tibetan religious history. When he was young he took up the practice of black magic in order to take revenge on the enemies of his family. Through the powers he gained practicing black magic he destroyed his enemies' crops and killed thirty-seven people. Then he realized the consequences of the evil deeds he had committed and decided to practice the Dharma in order to purify himself. He studied with different teachers and then met Marpa who became his root lama. Marpa subjected him to six years of arduous labor in order that he might be purified of the bad karma he had acquired through practicing black magic. At the end of this period of trial Marpa initiated him into the tantric maṇdalas. He then practiced in mountain caves, sometimes living for months on a diet of herbs. Because of the power of his Tummo (gTum Mo—Heat Yoga) he wore only a cotton cloth in the dead of the Himalayan winter. He had many disciples who attained realization. His two main disciples were Gampopa (also known as Dvags Po Lha rJe, the doctor from Dagpo, 1079–1153) and Rechungpa (Ras Chung Pa).

Gampopa's wife died when he was in his twenties and he decided to renounce the world and become a monk. He received the teachings of the Kadam tradition and of Milarepa and these two traditions merged within him. He obtained the supreme realization and became a great scholar. He wrote many scholarly texts, the most famous being the Dagpo'i Thargyen (Dvags Po'i Thar rGyan) in which the teachings of the Kadam tradition and those of Milarepa are combined. Because of the renown of Dagpo Lhaje's scholarship this school became known as the Dagpo Kagyud. From this original school, four major sub-schools and eight minor sub-schools developed. The four major sub-schools of the Kagyud are: Karma Kagyud (or Kamtsang Kagyud), Phagtru Kagyud, Tshalpa Kagyud and Barom Kagyud.

(1) Karma Kagyud (Karma bKa' rGyud). This school grew out of the disciples of Karmapa Tusum Khyenpa (Dus gSum mKyen Pa, 1110–1193). He studied with many teachers including Gampopa and Rechungpa, attained the supreme realization and built monasteries at Karma Lhading (Lha lDing) and Tshurphu (mTshur Phu). His incarnation was known as Karmapa Pakshi (1206–1283) and he was the first recognized incarnation or tulku (sPrul sKu) in Tibet. He visited the court of the Mongols who at that time ruled China and he became the chaplain of the emperor, who bestowed the title 'Karmapa Pakshi' on him. The Karmapa lineage is the head of this school and now is generally recognized as the head of the whole Kagyud lineage. The 16th Karmapa Rigpa'i Dorje (1924–1981) established his monastic headquarters in exile in Sikkim, India. In the last two decades Karmapa and his disciples established over 100 educational and meditational centers in the West. Since the passing away of the 16th Karmapa his regent, Zhamar Rinpoche, is presiding over this school.

The Karmapas are also known as the Black Hat Lamas because from the 1st or 2nd Karmapa (there is a scholarly dispute on this point) they have worn a black hat made from the hair of 10,000,000 dakinis. This hat, which is worn on ceremonial occasions, has been passed through the entire lineage of the Karmapas. In Tibet the main monastery of this lineage is Tshurpu located in the center of the country. The 3rd Karmapa, Rangchung Dorje (Rang Byung rDo rJe, 1284–1339), was a great siddha and scholar and the 8th Karmapa Mikyod Dorje (Mi bsKyod rDo rJe, 1507–1554) was a renowned writer.

This school produced many other great lamas. One of the most famous was Situ Chokyo Nagwa (Chos Kyi sNang Ba, 1700–1774), who built the great Kagyud monastery of Palpung (dPal sPung) in Dege, Kham, in 1727. He was also a great scholar and wrote fifteen texts including the famous commentary on the Tibetan grammatical root texts. While living in Palpung monastery the great nineteenth century scholar and writer Kongtrul Yonten Gyatsho (Kong sPrul Yon Ten rGya mTsho, 1813–1899) wrote and compiled 100 volumes of both Nyingma and Kagyud teachings. His works are known as the Dzod lNga)—the Five Treasures of Kongtrul.

The other lineages of highly venerated reincarnations of the Karma Kagyud are the Zhamarpa (Zha dMar Pa or Red Hat), Gyaltshab (rGyal Tshab), Situ and Nenang Pawo (gNas Nang dPa' Bo) Lamas.

(2) Phagtru Kagyud (Phag Gru bKa' brGyud). This school was founded by Phagmo Trupa Dorje Gyalpo (Phag Mo Gru Pa rDo rJe rGyal Po, 1110–1170). He took teachings from many teachers including Gampopa, who taught him the Mahāmudrā doctrine. He built a monastery at a place known as Phagmo (now called gDan Sa mThil) in southern Tibet and his tradition came to be known as Phagtru Kagyud. He had many disciples. Some of them were: Tag (sTag)-lung Thangpa, Na (sNa)-phupa, Ling Re Pema Dorje (gLing Ras Padma rDo rJe), Tsangpa Gyal Re Choje Jigten Gonpo (gTsang Pa rGyal Ras Chos rJe 'Jigs rTen mGon Po), Kalden Yeshe Sengye (sKal ldan Ye Shes Seng Ge), Ye Phugpa, Kyer Gompa (Gyer bsGom Pa) and Gyaltsha Rinpoche Kunden (lDan) Repa (Ras Pa). Many sub-schools developed from the disciples of Phagmo Trupa.

(3) Tshalpa Kargyud. This school was founded by Zhang Darma Trag (Grags) who was born in 1122. His main teacher was Wongom Tshulthrim Nyingpo (dBon bsGom Tshul Khrims sNying Po) who was a close disciple of Gampopa. He built the Gungthang monastery and had many disciples.

(4) Barom Kagyud ('Ba Rom bKa' brGyud). This school was founded by Darma Wangchung (dBang Phyung) of Barom in northern Tibet. He was a close disciple of Gampopa and attained great realization as a result of his teachings. He built the Barom monastery and thus his tradition is known as the Barom Kagyud.

The eight minor sub-schools of the Kagyud lineage all developed from the Phagtru Kagyud school. They were founded by disciples of Phagmo Trupa. They are outlined as follows.

(1) Drikung Kagyud ('Bri Gung bKa 'brGyud). This school was founded by Kyobpa Jigten Sumgon (1143–1217). He received the highest Kagyud teachings from Phagmo Trupa and became a great scholar and famous bhikṣu. When he gave teachings 55,000 people sometimes attended, including 10,000 monks. He built a monastery in the Drikung valley in central Tibet and his tradition is known as the Drikungpa. He wrote a series of scholarly volumes called the Gong Chig (sGongs gCig). The most famous scholar and writer in the later history of this tradition was Rinchen Phuntshogs (1509–1557) who wrote on aspects of both Nyingma and Kagyud teaching. There are still a large number of Drikung Kagyud followers and monasteries in Ladakh. The present heads of Drikung Kagyud are Kyabgon Chetsang (1946–),

who lives in Ladakh, and Kyabong Chungtshang (1942–), who is in Tibet.

(2) Taglung Kagyud (sTag Lung bKa' brGyud). Tralung Thangpa Trashi Pal (bKra Shis dPal, 1142–1210) founded this school. He was an attendant to Phagmo Trupa, received the complete teachings and attained the realized state of meditationless Mahāmudra. He built a monastery in the Taglung valley and his tradition was named after the valley. He had 3000 students. The famous scholar Ngagwang Tragpa (Nga dBang Grags Pa) was also instrumental in the development of this tradition. Sangye Wontragpa Pal (Sangs rGyas dBon Grags Pa dPal, 1251–1296), a nephew of Gampopa, built the Riwoche monastery in Kham. The monastery is noteworthy in that it contains different colleges for the study of the different schools in Tibetan Buddhism. The Zhabtrung Rinpoche who now lives in Sikkim, India, is the present head of the Taglung Kagyud.

(3) Yamzang Kagyud (gYam bZagn bKa' bryGyud). This school was founded by Phagmo Trupa's disciple Yeshe Senge. He received the highest realization just by seeing the Guru and listening to the introductory instructions in meditation. His chief disciple Yazangpa (gYa' bZang Pa) was born in 1169 and built the Yazang monastery. The tradition took its name from this monastery.

(4) Throphu Kagyud (Khro Phu bKa' brGyud). This tradition was founded by Rinpoche Gyaltsha and Kunden Repa (Kun lDan Ras Pa) who were brothers (some accounts say nephew and uncle) and disciples of Phagmo Trupa. Rinpoche Gyaltsha built the Throphu monastery. They had a nephew called Throphu Lotsawa—the translator from Throphu valley. He took teachings and the bhikṣu vows from his uncles and then went to Nepal and studied with many Indian teachers including the great Paṇḍita Śākyaśrī of Kashmir. He built an 80-foot statue of Maitri Buddha within the Throphu monastery and wrote many important texts.

(5) Shugseb Kagyud (Shugs gSeb bKa' brGyud). This tradition was founded by Phagmo Trupa's disciple Chokyi Senge, who built Nyephu Shugseb (sNye Phu Shugs gSeb) monastery. The school is named after this monastery.

(6) Yepa Kagyud (Yel Ba bKa' brGyud). This tradition was established by Yelwa Yeshe Tseg (Yel Ba Ye Shes brTsegs). He built the Shar Dorje Dang (Shar rDo rJe lDangs), Lho Yelphug and Chang Tana (Byang rTa rNa) monasteries.

(7) Martshang Kagyud (sMar Tshang). This tradition was started by

Marpa Rinchen Lodro (sMar Pa Rin Chen Blo Gros) of Mar Shod in Kham.

(8) Drugpa Kagyud ('Brug Pa bKa' brGyud). This tradition was established by Phagmo Trupa's highly realized disciple Ling Repa (gLing Ras Pa, 1128–1189) and the latter's disciple Tsangpa Gyare (gTsang Pa rGya Ras, 1161–1211). This school eventually divided into three sub-schools known as the Middle (or Central) Drugpa, Lower Drugpa and Upper Drugpa Kagyud. Each of these three branches is briefly discussed below.

(a) The Pardrug (Bar 'Brug)—Middle Drugpa Kagyud. Long Repa was a highly realized disciple of Phagmo Trupa who had many disciples and who constructed a monastery at Na(sNa)-phur. His disciple Tsangpa Gyare became a famous teacher whose teachings were sometimes attended by as many as 50,000 people. After building the Longbol (kLong rBol) and Ralung monasteries he went to a place called Nam (gNam)-gyi Phu to build a monastery. When he and his party reached Namgyi Phu they saw nine roaring dragons flying in the sky. The Tibetan word for dragon is ''Brug' which is pronounced as 'Drug'. The flying dragons were taken to be an auspicious omen and the monastery and the lineage which sprang from it came to be known as the Drugpa. This school eventually became very popular in Tibet. Its followers were simple people, content with few material possessions, who were known for their deep practice of the dharma. There is a Tibetan proverb which says:

> Half of the people are Drugpa Kagyudpas,
> Half of the Drugpa Kagyudpas are beggars,
> And half of the beggars are Drubthobs (Siddhas).

Later in this tradition many great scholars appeared including Sangye Dorje (Sangs rGyas rDo rJe), Pod Khepa (Bod mKhas Pa) and Padma Karpo (dKar Po). Padma Karpo (1527–1592) was a famous scholar whose collected works fill fourteen volumes. Among the Drukpa Kagyudpas he is known as Kun Khyen (Kun mKhyen-All Knowing). He was the fourth Drugchen incarnation of Tsangpa Gyare. He founded the Sangngag Choling (gSang sNgags Chos Gling) monastery near the Tibet-Indian border. This monastery became the residence of the Drugchen incarnations. Two lineages of incarnations came from him—Pagsam Wangpo (dPag bSam dBang Po) and Ngagwang Namgyal (Ngag dBang rNam rGyal, 1594–1651). The latter went to Bhutan and became both the spiritual and temporal head of the country. Eventually this school became very powerful in Bhutan and in the Tibetan and Bhutanese languages Bhutan is known as 'Drug Yul' or 'Country of the Dragon.'

The greatest siddhas of this school are Tsangnyon (gTsang sMyon, 1452–1507), Drugnyon Kunleg ('Brug sMyon Kun Legs, 1455–?) and Wynyon (dBus sMyon, 1458–?).

(b) The Meddrug (sMad 'Brug)—Lower Drugpa Kagyud. This sub-school was founded by Lorepa Darma Wangchug (Lo Ras Pa Dar Ma dBang Phyug) who was a disciple of Tsangpa Gyare. He lived a very humble and strictly disciplined life. He built the Wuri (dBu Ri) and Sengeri (Seng Ge Ri) monasteries. The tradition he founded is known as Meddrug.

(c) The Toddrug (sTod 'Brug)—Upper Drugpa Kagyud. This sub-school was founded by God Tsangpa Gonpo Dorje (rGod Tshang Pa mGon Po rDo rJe, 1189–1258), who was also an important disciple of Tsangpa Gyare. He was very highly realized, led a simple and austere life and had many disciples. His main disciples were Ogyenpa (O rGyan Pa), Yangonpa (Yang dGon Pa), Chilkarpa (sPyil dKar Pa) and Neringpa. Barawa Gyaltshen Palzang ('Ba' Ra Ba rGyal mTshan dPal bZang, 1255–1343) was one of the greatest scholars of this lineage. Ogyenpa Rinchenpal (1230–1309), who was a disciple of God Tshangpa, became a great siddha and visited Bodhagaya, Jalandara, Oḍḍiyana and China. He wrote many works including a famous guide to the Oddiyāna country. He had many disciples including the Karmapa Rangchung Dorje (Rang Byung rDo rJe), Kharchupa (mKhar Chu Pa, 1284–1339) and Togden Daseng (rTogs lDan Zla Seng). The 12th Drugchen Rinpoche, the present head of the Drugpa Kagyud, has established his monastic seat in exile in Darjeeling, India.

At the present time the best known of these sub-schools are the Karma Kagyud (or Karma Kamtshang), Drugpa Kagyud and Drikung Kagyud.

Some of the important monasteries of the Kagyud school are: Daglha Gampo, built by Gampopa in 1122; Densathil, built by Phagmo Trupa in 1158; Drikung Thil, built by Minyag Gomring in 1179; Taglung, built by Thangpa Trashipal in 1180; Ralung, built by Tsangpa Gyare in 1189; Tshurphu, built by Karmapa Tusum Khyenpa in 1189; Riwoche, built by Sangye Wontragpa; Sangngag Choling, built by Padma Karpo; and Palpung, built by Situ Chokyi Nangwa in 1727.

KAGYUD DOCTRINE

The Kagyud teachings are based on the Kadam tradition and the tantras of the New Translation. The special teachings of this school are the Naro Chodrug (Na Ro Chos Drug—Six Yogas of Nāropa) from the Indian Mahāsiddha Nāropa, and the Mahāmudrā teachings of Mahāsiddha Maitrīpa.

The Naro Chodrug (Six Yogas of Nāropa)

There are six aspects of this advanced Vajrayāna meditation practice. They are briefly described as follows.

(1) Tummo (gTum Mo, Heat Yoga). This is the basic practice of the Six Yogas of Nāropa in which the veins, air, heat and essence are used to produce the four kinds of bliss and to actualize the wisdom of the union of bliss and emptiness. The union of bliss and emptiness is known as the Mahāmudrā.

(2) Gyulu (sGyu Lus, Illusory Body). The purpose of this practice is to make further progress on the path of realization. Through the practice of this yoga the meditator is taught to see all appearance as the illusory body of the deities.

(3) Milam (rMi Lam, Dream). This yoga is used to test the strength of the practice. The meditator is trained to maintain awareness during sleep and dream states.

(4) Odsal ('OdgSal, Radiant Clarity). This practice is the essence of the path. The meditator practices until he achieves the state of the Unborn Radiant Clarity Samādhi in which all of existence becomes the spontaneously arising body of clarity and emptiness.

(5) Bardo (Bar Do, Intermediate State Between Death and Rebirth). This practice is used to actualize the union of clarity and emptiness in the intermediate state through the experience of the Illusory Body and Radiant Clarity.

(6) Phowa ('Pho Ba, Transference). This practice is used to maintain the continuity of the path throughout one's life. If the meditator should die before perfecting the path through this practice he is able to continue his practice into the next life. By this practice the meditator can enter the Pure State through the door of the Mahmudrā. There is another type of Phowa called "Pho Ba Grong 'Jug' which enables the

practitioner to transfer his consciousness into another body.

The lineage of this teaching came from the celestial Buddha Vajradhara, Mahāsiddha Tīlopa, Mahāsiddha Nāropa, the great translator Marpa, Milarepa and Gampopa, etc.

Mahāmudrā (Phyag rGya Chen Po)

The Mahāmudrā teachings have two aspects. The Muhāmudrā of Sūtra and the Mahāmudrā of Tantra.

In the Muhāmudra of Sūtra it is taught that the nature of mind is Radiant Clarity and undefiled. The meditator meditates directly on unmodified mind which is inseparable from appearances and emptiness. The Relative Truth is the sudden defilements and the Absolute Truth is the Buddha Nature. In reality, all existents are free from all conceptualization and are emptiness.

In the Mahāmudra of Tantra the meditator is introduced to the nature of mind and concentrates on that one-pointedly. As a result, the Lung (rLung, air or energy) enters the Wuma (dBu Ma—central vein) and generates the Tummo (gTum Mo, heat—Caṇḍalī, Skt.) and develops the four kinds of bliss. The meditator then concentrates on the union of bliss and emptiness in order to attain the final goal of the Mahāmudrā state.

The lineage of the Mahāmudra teachings came from the Indian Mahāsidda Maitrīpa and was introduced into Tibet by the translator Marpa who passed it to Milarepa who passed it to Gampopa. These teachings have been passed through an unbroken lineage of masters down to the present day.

The fundamental teachings of the various schools of the kagyud tradition are the same. However, the different schools had slightly different methods of practice and interpretation.

3

THE SAKYA SCHOOL

Grey Earth School

Khon Konchong Gyalpo ('Khon dKon mChong rGyal Po, 1034–1102) was the founder of this school. In 1073 he built a monastery in Upper Tsang. At the place where he built this monastery the color of the earth was grey. 'Sakya' means grey earth and the monastery and the tradition that came from it are known as Sakya.

The earlier generation of the Khon clan were noted followers of the Nyingma. But Khon Konchong Gyalpo went to the great translator Drogmi Sakya Yeshe ('Brog Mi Sakya Ye Shes, 993–1050) and received the teachings and initiations of the New Tantra (gSar Ma). He was instructed in the Lamdre (Lam 'Bras—the path and result) teachings which had been expounded by the Indian Mahāsiddha Bairupa.

Khon Konchong Gyalpo's son, Sachen Kunga Nyingpo (Sa Chen Kun dGa' sNying Po, 1092–1158) became a great scholar and Siddha. He received the special Lamdre teachings from Mahāsiddha Bairupa himself who came to the Sakya monastery by his miraculous power and stayed and taught for one month. Two of Sachen Kunga Nyingpo's sons, Sodnam Tsemo (bSod Nams rTse Mo, 1142–1182) and Tragpa Gyaltshen (Grags Pa rGyal mTshan, 1147–1216), became great scholars and Siddhas. Their younger brother's son, Kunga Gyaltshen (Kun dGa' rGyal mTshan, 1181–1251), became the greatest scholar of the Sakya school. He was recognized as the highest authority on the teachings of the lineage. He became a bhikṣu and wrote many scholarly volumes. Later he became known as the Sakya Paṇḍita. He defeated the great south Indian Pandit, Harinanda, in a debate in the Kyirong valley between Tibet and Nepal. He was invited to the Chinese court by the Mongolian emperor of China, Gotan, who was the grandson of Gengis Khan. He became the supreme teacher at the Chinese court.

The Sakya Paṇḍita's younger brother's older son, Drogon Chogyal

Phagpa ('Gro mGon Chos rGyal 'Phags Pa, 1235–1280), was a great teacher and became the first Lama ruler of Tibet. He studied under his uncle's guidance and became a highly realized Lama. After his uncle's death he became the guru to the Chinese emperor Kublai Khan. In return for receiving abhiṣeka (initiation) the emperor offered him thirteen Myriarchies (Khri sKor), comprising central, western and southern Tibet. At the time of his second visit to China he devised a script for the Mongolian language and it became known as 'Phagpa's script,' and the emperor offered him all three provinces (Chol Kha) of Tibetan territory. He thus became the ruler of Tibet and the Sakyapas controlled the country for a century after AD 1253.

The Sakya school produced many great scholars throughout its long history in Tibet. Its five greatest scholars are known as the Sakya Gongma Namga (Sa sKya Gong Ma rNam lNga), the five Supreme Ones of the Sakya. They were the Sakya Pandit, Sachen, Sodnam, Tragpa and Phagpa. Some of the other great scholars of the school are Yagtrug (gYag Phrug), Rongton (Rong sTon), Ngorpa, Dzongpa (rDzong Pa), Go Rabjam (Go Rab 'Byams) and Sakya Chogden (mChog lDan, 1428–1507). Go Rabjam Sodnam Senge (bSod Nams Seng Ge, 1429–1489) is one of the most famous writers of the Sakya. He is known as Kunkhyen (Sarvajña, Skt.) which means All Knowing. He wrote fifteen famous books.

In addition to the main Sakya school there are two sub–schools of this lineage: Ngorpa and Tsharpa. Ngorchen Kunga Zangpo (Ngor Chen Kun dGa' bZang Po, 1382–1456) built the Ngor E-Wam Choden (E Wam Chos lDan) monastery and it eventually became the second greatest Sakya monastery and a sub-school of the main lineage. The followers of another great teacher, Tshalchen Losal Gyatsho (Tshal Chen bLo gSal rGy mTsho, 1502–1566) established another sub-school which became known as the Tsharpa.

Since the lineage was founded, the primacy of the Sakya lineage has been passed through the Khon clan. They are also the heads of the main Sakya monastery. The present head of the Sakya school, the 41st throne-holder is Thri Rinpoche Kinga Thrinle Wangyal (Khri Rin Po Che Kun dGa' 'Phrin Las dBang rGyal), who was born in 1945 and lives in India.

In addition to the Sakya and Ngor monasteries in Tsang, the other important monasteries are: Lhundrub Teng in Dege province, built by Thangtong Gyalpo (1385–1509); Nalentra in Phanyul, built by Rongton Shecha Kunzig in 1436; Tanag, the seat of Go Rabjam (1429–1489); Dondrub Ling in Ga, built by Sherab Gyaltshen (1436–1486); Thupten

Serdog, the seat of Sakya Chogden (1428–1507); Dzongsar Trashi Lhatse in Kham; and Deur Chode, built by Chotrag Zangpo in Amdo.

SAKYA DOCTRINE

The special teaching of this school is the Lamdre teachings or the Path and Result. The view of Lamdre is the union of 'Clarity and Emptiness free from apprehensions' or 'the inseparability of samsāra and nirvāṇa.' Within the Lamdre teachings there are two aspects: Sūtra and Tantra.

A Sutra

Within the Sūtric aspect there are two traditions: (1) Nagārjuna and (2) Maitrinatha.

(1) Nāgārjuna. This tradition teaches the three Dogpa (bZlog Pa) practices. Dogpa means to reverse. These three practices are:

(a) By meditating on the suffering of samsāra, the difficulties of obtaining a human birth, the law of karma and maitri (loving-kindness) one will reverse oneself from unvirtuous actions.

(b) First, reflecting on the grasping of one's own body, to examine as follows: if the body is real, then it should be real from the beginning and independent of any causes and conditions. But the body has developed and functions only because of causes and conditions. By knowing this one will develop the certainty that the body is without reality. By meditating on this, one will cease to take the conceptualizations of grasping self as truth (Satyagrahaṇa) and will reverse the concept of Self-Grasping (grasping self or ego as true).

(c) Then one ceases to reflect on no-truth (Asatya): one will reverse the view of no-truth by recognizing that emptiness is free from grasping at an object; by recognizing that whether phenomena exist or do not exist is beyond the conception of the mind; and by dwelling in the state free from conceptualization and grasping.

(2) Maitrinatha. This tradition teaches that the natural Clarity-Wisdom of the Basis is the foundation of both samsāra and nirvāṇa. By not recognizing this, we are in delusion and are grasping as true the dual appearances of subject and object.

This delusion is the root of samsāra, and the purpose of the path is to destroy this ignorance by dissolving that duality into the ultimate sphere (Dharamdhātu).

B Tantra

The tantric aspect of the Lamdre teachings is used for the realization of the nature of the mind. First, one should recognize the ordinary mind and then meditate on its union of clarity and emptiness. From this practice one can find the Mind of natural wisdom spontaneously arisen and meditate on the meaning of it. Through this practice the mind will not be distracted by delusions. All appearances then arise as the play of wisdom. If deluded reflections still arise, then by recollection and mindfulness the delusory appearances transform themselves into the Nature of Wisdom.

The lineage of the Lamdre teachings came through the Indian teachers Virūpa, Pūrvakṛiṣṇa, Damarupa, Avadhuta and Gayadhara to the Tibetan translator Drogmi Yeshe. He passed it on to Khon Konchong Gyalpo, who taught it to his son. These teachings have come down to the present time through an unbroken lineage of teachers.

4

THE GELUG (dGe Lugs) SCHOOL

The Virtuous One

This school was founded by the celebrated scholar Tsongkhapa Lobzang Tragpa (Tsong Kha Blo bZang Grags Pa, 1357–1419). He built the Gaden (dGa'lDan) monastery in 1410 and the school was first known as Gadenpa and later as the Gelugpa.

Tsongkhapa was born in the Tsongkha valley in the Amdo province of eastern Tibet. He received the first precepts from the third Karmapa, Rolpa'i Dorje (Rol Pa'i rDo rJe, 1340–1383) and Choje Dondrub Rinchen (Chos rJe Don Grub Rin Chen). At the age of 16 he went to central Tibet to further his studies. He took bhiksu ordination in the lineage of Śākyaśrī of Kashmir. He studied the Madhyamaka and Adhibharma teachings with Redawa Zhonnu Lodro (Re mDa' Ba GZhon Nu Blo Gros) of the Sakya school. He received instruction in the tantras from Kyungpo Lhepa (Khyung Po Lhas Pas), a disciple of Puton (Bu sTon), and Lhotragpa Namkha Gyaltshen (Lho Brad Pa Nam mKha' rGyal mTshan). He had great aptitude for scholarship and during his life he wrote 210 treatises collected in twenty volumes. His most famous works are the Lamrin Chenmo (The Stages of the Path) and the Ngagrim Chenmo (The Stages of the Path of Tantra).

Philosophically, Tsongkhapa followed the Prāsaṅgika Madhyamaka teachings and the New Translation Tantras (gSang sNgags gSar Ma). The type of practice he emphasized was also deeply influenced by the style of the old Kadam school founded by Atīśa (982–1054) in Tibet. The Gelugpas are sometimes called the New Kadam School. He emphasized strict monastic discipline in the monasteries. Only celibate persons are admitted to Gelug monasteries and the clerical community.

Tsongkhapa had hundreds of great disciples. His two main disciples were Gyaltshab Je (rGyal Tshab rJe) and Khedrub Je (mKhas Grub rJe). Gyaltshab Darma Rinchen (rGyal Tshab Dar Maa Rin Chen,

1364–1432) wrote works in eight volumes and Khedrub Geleg Palzang (mKhas Grub dGe Legs dPal bZang, 1385–1438) wrote ten volumes on both sūtra and tantra. Some of his other main disciples were Duldzin Tragpa Gyaltshen ('Dul 'Dzin Grags Pa rGyal mTshan, 1374–?), Penchen Gedentrub (Pan Chen dGe 'Dun Grub, the First Dalai Lama, 1391–1474), Jamyang Choje ('Jam dByangs Chos rJe, 1379–1449), Chamchen Choje (Byams Chen Chos rJe, 1354–1435), Med Sherab Zangpo (sMad Shes Rab bZang Po) and Gyudchen Sherab Senge (rGyud Chen Shes Rab Seng Ge).

After Tsongkhapa's death, the holder of the throne of Gaden monastery (dGa' lDan Khri Pa) was Gyaltshab Je and then Khedrub Je. Since that time the throne-holders of Gaden have been the seniormost scholars and they are the heads of the Gelug school. The present 98th throne-holder of Gaden, the head of the Gelug school, is Thrichen Jampal Zhenphen ('Jam dPal gZhan Phan, 1921–), who officiates in exile in India.

GELUG MONASTERIES

The Gelugpas constructed huge monastic establishments in many parts of Tibet. Some of the most important ones were as follows.

(1) Gaden Monastery. This monastery was built by Tsongkhapa himself in 1409. It is located twenty-five miles from Lhasa and had residences for 4000 monks. It had two major colleges (Gra Tshangs) for study of both sūtra and tantra.

(2) Drepung ('Bras sPung) Monastery. This monastery was built by Tsongkhapa's disciple Jamyang Choje in 1416. It is located three miles west of Lhasa and had accommodation for 9000 monks. It had three colleges for the study of sūtra and one college for the study and practice of tantra.

(3) Sera Monastery. This monastery was built by Tsongkhapa's disciple Chamchen Choje in 1419. It is located 1½ miles north of Lhasa and had accommodation for 7000 monks. It had two colleges for sūtra study and one for tantra.

(4) Trashi Lhunpo (bKra Shis Lhun Po). This monastery was built by Penchen Geduntrub, the 1st Dalai Lama, in 1447. It had residences for 4000 monks and three colleges for sūtra study and one for tantra. It was the seat of the Dalai Lamas until the 1st Panchen Lama became head of the monastery. The first Panchen Lama Lobzang Chokyi

Gyaltshen (Blo bZang Chos Kyi rGyal mTshan, 1570–1662) was one of the greatest Gelug scholars and the tutor of the 5th Dalai Lama. Since his time this monastery has been the seat of the Panchen Lamas. The present Panchen Lama was born in 1938 and is now in China.

(5) Gyudmed Tratshang (rGyud sMad Gra Tshang—Lower Tantric Training college). This monastice college is located in Lhasa and was founded by Sherab Senge, a disciple of Tsongkhapa, in 1440. It had accommodation for 500 tantric bhikṣus.

(6) Gyutod Tratshang (rGyud sTod Gra Tshang–Upper Tantric Training College). This monastic college was founded by Kunga Dontrub (Kun dGa' Grub), a disciple of Sherab Senge, in 1474. It was a training college for 900 tantric bhikṣus.

(7) Chabdo (Chab mDo) Monastery. This monastery is located in the Kham province of eastern Tibet. It was built by Tsongkhapa's disciple Chamchen Choje in 1437.

(8) Kubum (sKu 'Bum) Monastery. This monastery is located in the Amdo province of eastern Tibet at the birthplace of Tsongkhapa. It was built with the advice and blessing of the 3rd Dalai Lama, Sodnam Gyatsho (bSod Nams rGya mTsho, 1543–1588). It had residences for 3700 monks and had three colleges. One of the colleges was for medicine and the other two were for sūtric and tantric study and practice.

(9) Trashi Gomang (bKra Shis sGo Mang) Monastery. This monastery was built in 1710 by Jamyang Zhedpa Ngangwang Tsondru ('Jam dByangs bZhad Pa Ngag Bang brTson 'Grus, 1648–1721), a disciple of the 5th Dalai Lama. It is located in the Amdo province of eastern Tibet and had residences for 3700 monks. Many great scholars have come from this monastery such as Gongthang Tenpa'i Dronme (Gong Thang bsTan Pa'i sGron Me). It had four colleges: one for sūtra, two for tantra and one for medicine.

(10) Gonlung (dGon Lung) Monastery. This monastery was built by Donyod Chokyi Gyatsho (Don Yod Chos Kyi rGya mTsho) in the Amdo province of eastern Tibet in 1592. From this monastery the great Changkya (Chang sKya) and Thukvan (Thu bKvan) incarnations spread the Gelug teachings into Mongolia and parts of China. Many Buddhist scriptures were translated from Tibetan into Mongolian and Chinese at this monastery.

(11) Riwo Gegyeling (Ri Bo dGe rGyas Gling or Ta Khu Ral) Monastery. This monastery was located in Hal Ha, Outer Mongolia, and was founded by the 1st Jetsun Dampa, Lobzang Tenpa'i Gyaltsen (rJe bTsun Dam Pa, Blo bZang bsTan Pa'i rGyal mTshan, 1635–1723),

who was an incarnation of Taranath. The Jetsun Dampa was the highest lama in Mongolia and occupied a position comparable to that of the Dalai Lama in Tibet. This monastery was his residence. It had 27,000 monks and eleven colleges.

There were also hundreds of large and small Gelug monasteries in Mongolia before the coming of the communists. In addition there were also a few Gelug monasteries in China before 1949.

GELUG DOCTRINE

The Gelugpas are proponents of the Prāsaṅgika Madhyamaka philosophical tradition and they largely adopted the method of practice taught by Atīśa in the Kadam system. Their tantric teachings, from the New Translation of the tantras, are the Kriyāyoga Tantra, Caryāyoga Tantra, Yoga Tantra and Anuttarayoga Tantra. The method of the Kadam school is summarized in the following passage:

> To accept all the doctrine (of Buddha) as instructions, to understand that all the instructions are the main path (or part of the path) that leads a person to the attainment of Buddhahood, and to practice the three stages of the path (higher, middle and lesser) according to one's own capacity.

The Gelupas stress the teaching on interdependent arising to prove that all things are empty and free from conceptualization. According to the doctrine of interdependent arising, all phenomena are without self-nature and arise because of mutually interdependent causes and conditions. Thus phenomena are empty in that they lack self-nature and do not function independently of one another.

The Gelugpas practice both the sūtras and tantras according to the method of the 'Stages of the Path,' which is a gradual method beginning with the Preliminary Practices and ending with the Perfection of Transcendental Wisdom. In their tantric practice they use two stages (Rim gNyis): development (bsKyed Rim) and perfection (rDzogs Rim). Through the use of this method they realize emptiness through the spontaneously arising bliss and attain fully perfected Buddhahood.

The deep and intensive study of the Buddhist scriptures is strongly emphasized by the Gelug school. For the study of sūtra the following texts are mainly used: (1) the Nyāya (logic) texts of Dignāga and Dharmakīrti; (2) Prajñāramitā of Maitrinatha and Asaṅgha; (3) the Madhyamaka texts of Nāgārjuna and Candrakīrti; (4) the Adhidharma of Vasubandhu and Asaṅgha; and (5) the Vinaya text of Guṇaprabha. In addition to the original texts, many commentaries by both Indian and Tibetan scholars are studied. For example, just considering Drepung monastery alone, each Tratshang (college) has a different Yigcha (commentarial texts) written by Gelug scholars of their own Tratshang. The study of the original texts is done on the basis of these commentaries. The following tantras are mainly studied: Guhyasamāja, Cakrasaṁvara, Vajrabhairava, Hevajra, Kālacakra and Vajrayoginī.

The following quotations from the works of Tsongkhapa give an indication of the main points of the Gelug teachings. In the Drangne Legshed Nyingpo (Drangs Nges Legs bShad sNying Po) he says,

> By the assertion of the inevitable interdependent
> arising of saṃsāra and nirvaṇa,
> Destroy all the characteristic conceptualizations;
> By the moon-like teachings of Candrakīrti,
> When the Kumud garden-like mind and eyes have opened,
> By seeing the path shown by Buddhapālita,
> who will not hold the excellent philosophy of
> Nāgārjuna as supreme?

In the Lamtso Namsum (Lam gTso rNam gSum—the Three Principal Aspects of the Path), he says,

> If you do not have the wisdom of realizing the nature
> (real state),
> Even if you have gained the experience of revulsion from
> saṃsāra and have generated Bodhicitta,
> You cannot cut the root of saṃsāra;
> So try the means of understanding interdependent arising
> (pratītyasamutpāda).
>
> Whoever sees that the functioning of cause and result
> Of all the existents of saṃsāra and nirvāṇa is inevitable
> And destroys all conceptualization,
> Enters the path 'Pleasing to the Buddha.'
>
> As long as you see the two—
> Appearances, the inevitable interdependent arising,
> And emptiness, the non-assertion (of its existence)—
> as separate,
> You still do not understand the vision of the Buddha.
>
> When simultaneously without alternative,
> You just realize that interdependent arising is inevitable,

It destroys all grasping at the objects of conception;
Then the analysis of the Darśan (view) is complete.

5

SOME OTHER TIBETAN BUDDHIST SCHOOLS

(1) KADAM (bKa' gDams) SCHOOL

The great Indian scholar Atīśa Dīpaṁkaraśrījñāna (982–1055) founded this school. He was an abbot of Vikramaśīla Monastic University, which was one of the three greatest centers of Buddhist learning during his time in India. He was invited to Tibet in 1042 by Yeshe Od (Ye Shes 'Od) and Changchub Od who were closely related to the dynasty of the early dharma kings of Tibet. He gave many teachings of the Buddhist sūtras and instructions for correctly practicing the teachings. He wrote the famous text 'The Light of the Path.' In this short work he explained all the Buddha's teachings as one path, dividing it into three parts for persons of higher, middle and lesser intelligence. He lived and taught in Tibet for seventeen years until the time of his death.

His renowned disciple Dromton ('Brom sTon, 1004–1064) built the Radreng (Ra bsGreng) monastery to the north of Lhasa and it became the source of the Kadam teachings. Dromton's three principal disciples were Potowa (Po To Ba), Phuchungwa (Phu Chung Ba) and Chenngawa (sPyan sNga Ba). The Kadampas emphasized strict and earnest ascetic practice and full understanding of the meaning of the teachings. Their teachings are simple and mostly in local dialects but are deep and full of meaning and inspiration.

A separate school did not survive but their teachings and parables deeply influenced the other schools of Tibetan Buddhism. This is because most of the original Kadampas were hermits and did not build monasteries. Their followers, however, did construct monasteries and these became the foundation of the Kagyud, Gelug and other schools. Gelugpas call themselves the New Kadampas and the Kagyudpas say that their teachings are the confluence of the Mahāmudrā and Kadam.

(2) ZHICHED (Zhi Byed) and CHOD (gCod)

Zhiched means 'pacification' or the 'doctrine which pacifies suffering.' This lineage was founded in Tibet by the great south Indian Saint Phadampa Sangye. He visited Tibet on five occasions, the last time being in 1098 after his return from China.

His teachings were based on the Prajñāpāramitā Sūtras and the philosphy of Nāgārjuna. The distinctive aspect of Phadampa Sangye's teaching was the method he used to pacify suffering. In most types of teaching the defilements which are the cause of suffering are first purified and then the suffering is dissolved. But in this method the suffering is first purified, and thereupon the defilements which are its cause are eliminated. In this practice the suffering itself is used as a practice. The teaching of this lineage went through three periods of development marked by Phadampa Sangye's different visits to Tibet.

The teachings of Chod are a major practice of this school. Chod means 'to cut off,' specifically to cut off the ego and defilements which are the root of saṃsāra. There are two types of Chod:

(a) **Pho Chod** (male Chod), and

(b) **Mo Chod** (female Chod). The practice of Mo Chod is the most popular.

(a) **Pho Chod.** This teaching was transmitted by Phadampa Sangye to Kyoton Sodnam (sKyo sTon bSod Nams) and Mara Serpo (sMa Ra Ser Po) who in turn transmitted it to Nyonpa Serang (sMyon Pa Se Rong), Tseton (rTse sTon) and Sumton (Sum sTon).

(b) **Mo Chod.** This lineage was transmitted by Kyoton Sodnam to the great female saint Machig Labdron (sGron, 1031–1129). She is recognized by all Tibetan schools as a Wisdom Dākinī in human form. Because of her influence the Chod teachings were established in the different schools in all parts of Tibet and have been passed down to the present time. There were numerous Chod texts and teachings that came from her in different forms. Many of them were discovered as Dharma Treasures (gTer). She spent the last years of her life in a cave at Zangri Kharmar (Zangs Ri mKhar dMar) in southern Tibet.

Both Chod teachings are based on the Prajnāāpāramitā Sūtras. The basic practice is to purify the defilements by completely cutting off grasping at self, which is the root of saṃsāra. The Six Pāramitās (perfections) are practiced by giving away one's own body and possessions to all including the most fearful beings in dangerous places without attachment, fear or doubt. Machig Labdron divided the Chod into three aspects:

> To travel to dangerous and solitary places is the
> Outer Chod,
> To transform the body as food for demons is the
> Inner Chod,
> To cut off the single thing (grasping) from the root
> Is the Actual Chod.
> Whoever practices these three Chods is a yogi.

At present there is no separate lineage of this tradition but its teachings are practiced in all the schools, especially in the Nyingma and Kagyud.

(3) JONANG (Jo Nang) SCHOOL

This lineage was founded in Tibet by Yumo Mikyod Dorje (Yu Mo Mi bsKyod rDo rJe) who was a great teacher of the Kalacakra Tantra. He attained a profound realization of the meaning of emptiness, which is called other-emptiness (gZhan sTon). Kunpang Thugje Tshondru (Kun sPang Thugs rJe brTson 'Grus, 1243–?), who was a holder of this lineage, built a monastery at Jomonang and it became the source of the Jonang teachings. His great disciple, Dolpho Sherab Gyaltshen (Dol Bo Shes Rab rGyal mTshan, 1292–1361) became a very famous scholar of his time. He expounded the Zhantong philosophy in his Richo Ngedon Gyatsho (Ri Chos Nges Don rGya mTsho) and Kadu Zhipa (bKa'bsDu bZhi Pa). According to his teaching the universal ground (Kun bZhi) has two parts: wisdom and sense. Wisdom is the absolute truth of Buddha nature which is true, pure, eternal and exists in all beings. But because of the delusion of the senses, this undifferentiated, pure natural state is obscured. Through the practice of the 'Six Yogas' taught by the Jonangpas, the obscurations of the senses are removed and the absolute state is attained. The disciples of this school mainly rely on Dolpo Sherab Gyaltshen's works for study and practice. His most famous disciples were Sazang Mati Rinchen (Sa bZang Ma Ti Rin Chen) and Potong Chogle Namgyal (Po Tong Phyogs Las rNam rGyal, 1360–1386). In later centuries Kunga Trolchog and Tāranātha (1575?) were great teachers and scholars of this lineage. However, in the seventeenth century, because of political difficulties, this school ceased to function actively in central Tibet, but it remained powerful in eastern Tibet until recent times. The Shardzamthang (Shar 'Dzam Thang) monastery built by Kazhipa Rinchenpal (Ka bZhi Pa Rin Chen dPal) in 1665 in Golok province became the unofficial center of the Jonang tradition in recent centuries.

The scriptures and meditation practices of the Tibetan lineages differ from one another according to their origins in the various transmissions from India and the varying needs of their disciples in Tibet. Yet all these schools are the same in the crucial sense of directly or indirectly leading to the same goal. Enlightenment. Similarly, different medicines are the same in the sense that they all make people healthy.

PART II

The Scope of Tibetan Literature

INTRODUCTION

For many centuries the teachings of Buddhism deeply influenced all aspects of Tibetan life and culture. Many monks and high Lamas meditated on the teachings of the Buddha, Bodhisattvas and Siddhas and wrote extensively on all facets of the Buddha's Dharma. Eventually the discipline of Buddhism permeated all levels of Tibetan society and set the tone for the whole life of the people. Thus, any discussion about the life, history, culture and literature of Tibet must take Buddhism into account as a predominating factor. This is especially true for Tibetan literature because literary Tibetan was developed mainly in the seventh century AD for the purpose of translating the Buddhist scriptures into Tibetan.

In the intellectual world beyond the confines of Tibetan society, the Tibetan language is important because of the richness and vastness of the Buddhist literature contained within its scope. Today it is one of the four major Buddhist languages. The others are Sanskrit, Pali and Chinese.

The main treasury of Buddhist literature in India until the twelfth century AD was written in Sanskrit. It is an especially important source for the Mahāyāna; unfortunately, due to historical circumstances many of these priceless original Sanskrit texts were lost.

Pali, the ancient language of Magadha, was the major medium and source for Hinayāna Buddhist literature. In later centuries the rich treasury of Hinayāna scripture was preserved in the Theravadin countries. Especially important are the Tripiṭaka and the Aṭṭakathā, the huge commentary of the Tripiṭaka written by Ācārya Buddhaghoṣa.

Beginning in the early centuries of our era, many Buddhist texts were translated into Chinese, and on this foundation Chinese became a major source of Buddhist literature. But compared to Tibetan Buddhist literature, Professor Nalinakṣa Dutt has written, 'The Tibetan collection of translations of Indian texts is much larger than the Chinese. In a comparison made by Prof. Sakai Shinten between the Tibetan and Chinese versions of the Indian texts, he finds the Chinese translations are wanting in 670 texts of the Kajur and 3452 of the Tenjur.' He further said, 'One of the most outstanding contributions made by Tibetan scholars was the preservation of Sanskrit texts in literal and accurate Tibetan translations, in which they surpassed the Chinese in accuracy and volume.'

Thus it can be said that the Tibetan language contains the richest collection of Buddhist literature in the world today. All aspects of the Buddhist tradition—Hinayāna, Mahāyāna and Vajrayāna—are contained within its scope. The translation and exposition of the Buddha's Dharma formed the basis of literary Tibetan. Buddhism became the fountainhead of Tibetan literature and the main source of Tibetan cultural life.

Tibetan Literature

We will classify Tibetan literature into two broad divisions: Religious and secular. Although there was very little literature that was not influenced by religious concepts, there are many texts whose main subject matter deals with non-religious subjects such as grammar, medicine and law. Here these works are classified within the secular literature. Only works which deal primarily with religious themes are placed in the category of religious literature.

1

THE RELIGIOUS LITERATURE

The religious literature can be classified in two ways: (A) according to origin, and (B) according to subject. According to origin, there is first of all (1) a large body of literature translated from Indian sources into Tibetan. Secondly (2) there is the enormous volume of religious works written by Tibetan scholars. According to subject, the religious literature falls into four divisions: Religion; History and biography; Poetic composition and yogic songs; and Art, music and dance.

A RELIGIOUS LITERATURE—ACCORDING TO ORIGIN

1 The literature translated from Indian sources

(a) The Kajur Collection—the Buddha's teachings

The Kajur (bKa' 'Gyur) contains the scriptures of both sūtras and tantras. Although many of the sūtras were translated in the period of the Later Spread of the Doctrine (bsTan Pa Phyi Dar), most of them were translated into Tibetan during the Earlier Spread of the Doctrine (bsTan Pa sNga Dar) and revised during the period of the Later Spread. Most of the tantras contained in the Kajur are New Tantras (gSang sNgags gSar Ma) but there are also a few scriptures of the Old Tantra in this collection. The New Tantras are those which were translated beginning with Lochen Rinchen Zangpo (bZang Po, 958–1051). The Old Tantras are the tantric scriptures translated from the seventh century AD until the time of Ācārya Smṛtijñāna at the beginning of the eleventh century. Most of the Old Tantras are contained in the

Nyingma Gydbum (rNying Ma rGyud 'Bum) collection. The contents of the Kajur are as shown in Table II.1.

Table II.1 The Kajur Collection

No.	*Title of the sub-divisions*	*No. of vol.**	*No. of treatises**
1	rGyud (Tantra)	24	729
2	Sher Phyin (Prajñāpāramitā)	23	30
3	dKon brTsegs (Ratnakūṭa)	6	1
4	Phal Chen (Avataṃsaka)	6	1
5	mDo (Sūtra)	32	269
6	'Dul Ba (Vinaya)	13	16
		104	1046
7	The collection of rNying Ma rGyud 'Bum (Prācīn Tantras)	33†	375†

* These figures based on Peking edition.
† These figures based on Delhi publication.

Table II.2 The Tenjur Collection

No.	*Title of the sub-divisions*	*No. of vol.**	*No. of treatises**
1	bsTod Tshogs (Stotras)	½	63
2	rGyud 'Grel (Tantraṭīkā)	85½	3120
3	Sher Phyin (Prajñāpāramitā)	16	40
4	dBu Ma (Madhyamaka)	17	257
5	mDo 'Grel (Sūtraṭīkā)	10	40
6	Sems Tsam (Cittamātra Yogacarya)	18	45
7	mNgon Pa (Abhidharma)	11	19
8	'Dul Ba (Vinaya)	18	66
9	sKyes Rabs (Jātakamālā)	3½	8
10	sPring Yig (Lekha)	½	42
11	Thun Mong and Ngo mTshar bsTan bCos(Sādhārana Śāstra)	5 (out of 12½)	86 (out of 143)
		185	3786

* These figures based on Peking edition.

(b) The Tenjur Collection—the works of Indian Buddhist scholars

The Tenjur (bsTan 'Gyur) is the collection of commentarial texts written by ancient Indian Buddhist scholars on the Hinayāna, Mahāyana, and Tantra and translated into Tibetan. The Tenjur also contains texts on secular subjects and these are included within the secular literature section. The Dharma literature of the Tenjur is classified according to the sub-divisions shown in Table II.2.

2 The literature written by Tibetan scholars

There is a vast literature written by thousands of learned Tibetan scholars and sages on various aspects of Buddhism. This literature primarily concerns itself with the interpretation and explanation of the sūtras, tantras and commentaries written by great Indian scholars.

In order to understand this indigenous literature, it is necessary to know something about the Buddhist schools which developed in Tibet. These schools developed from the experience and wisdom of renowned Tibetan scholars and sages, and from the literary expression of their understanding.

In Tibet four major and many minor Buddhist schools developed. The four major schools are: Nyingma, Kagyud, Sakya and Gelug. The main division between these schools is in relation to the tantras, although there were also different interpretations of the sūtras among these schools. The followers of the Old Tantras or Earlier Translation (sNga' 'Gyur) are known as the Nyingmapa or Old Ones. The followers of the later translated tantras (Phyi 'Gyur) are known as the Sarmapa or New Ones. The Kagyud, Sakya and Gelug lineages are all within the Sarma tradition of tantra. In the following discussion of the literature produced by these schools, a few of the special features of each are pointed out.

(a) The literature of the Nyingma school

(i) The classification of the Dharma

The Nyingma classifies the whole Buddhist doctrine into Nine Yānas:

The Three Yānas of Pāramitā or Sūtra are:

(a) Śravakayāna (Hinayāna)

(b) Pratyekabuddhayāna (Hinayāna)
(c) Bodhisattva (Mahāyāna)

The Three Outer Tantras of Vajrayāna are:
(a) Kriyāyoga
(b) Caryāyoga
(c) Yogatantra

The Three Inner Tantras of Vajrayāna are:
(a) Mahāyoga
(b) Anuyoga
(c) Atiyoga

(ii) Sūtra

The original texts and commentaries are contained in the Kajur and Tenjur.

(iii) Tantra

There are some tantras contained in the Kajur and Tenjur from both the Earlier and Later periods of translation which are common to all schools. But the different schools would emphasize certain tantras, and these scriptures became special aspects of practice for a particular lineage. The special tantras of the Nyingma are the scriptures of the Mahāyoga, Anuyoga and Atiyoga (or rDzogs Pa Chen Po). Most of these teachings are contained within the Old Tantra collection (rNying Ma rGyud 'Bum). The three major divisions of the Old Tantra are: bKa' Ma (Canon), gTer Ma (concealed Dharma Treasures), and Dag sNang (Pure Vision).

(1) Kama (bKa' Ma). These tantras are the Three Inner Tantras translated into Tibetan by Guru Padmasambhava, Paṇḍita Vimalamitra, and others in the ninth century AD, and transmitted through an unbroken lineage of Lamas to the present day. Some of the major works within this division of Tantra are:

Mahayoga: (a) Tantra – The Māyājāla Tantra (sGyu 'Phrul Drva Ba) and eighteen Great Tantras (Tantra Chen Po sDe bCo brGyad) and
(b) Sādhana – Scriptures of Sādhanas of Eight Great Maṇḍalas.

Anuyoga: The Tantras of 'Dus Pa mDo

Atiyoga: The eighteen Tantras (Sems sMad bCo brGyad) of Sems sDe, nine Tantras (Klong dGu) of Klong sDe, and seventeen Tantras (bCu bDun rGyud) of Man Ngag sDe.

Compiled Kama texts: Minling Terchen (sMin Gling gTer Chen), Minling Lochen (sMin Gling Lo Chen) and Gyalsre Zhenphen Thaye (rGyal Sras gZhan Phan mTha' Yas) compiled many of the Kama texts. Later in some monasteries annual sādhana rituals of the Thirteen Kama Sādhana (bKa' Ma'i mChod Khang bCu gSum) were performed in assembly. The thirteen Sādhanas are: (1) 'Dus Pa mDo, (2) sGyu 'Phrul Zhi Khro, (3) Sangs rGyas mNyam sByor, (4) rTa mChog Rol Ba, (5) Na Rag Dong sPrungs, (6) gShin rJe gShed Ru mTshon dMar Nag, (7) Yang Dag So Lugs and Sa Lugs, (8) Phur Pa Rong Lugs, Rog Lugs and Sa Lugs, (9) Lung Lugs Tshe sGrub, (10) Guru Drag dMar 'O Bran Lugs, (11) rGyud mGon legs LDan, (12) sMin Gling rDor Sems and (13) Cha gSum (the last two are additional texts).

(2) Terma (gTer Ma). Many esoteric scriptures and teachings of Guru Padmasambhava were concealed by the Guru himself for the benefit of future disciples. He transmitted various teachings to his disciples and concealed them in the enlightened nature of their minds by the enlightened power of Guru Rinpoche, Ḍākinī Yeshe Tshogyal (Ye Shes mTsho rGyal), and others, to be discovered by future disciples. They were discovered in later centuries by the Hundred Great Tertons (Dharma Treasure Discoverers) and many other Tertons. The discovery of these teachings began with Terton Sangye Lama and Trapa Ngonshechen (Grva Pa mNgon Shes Can, 1012–1090) and has continued until the present day. There are two kinds of Termas: S Ter and Gong Ter.

(a) S Ter (Sa gTer). It is common to Sa Ter and Gong Ter that when the time comes and conditions are perfect the Tertons withdraw the teachings from the enlightened nature of their minds. Therein, centuries before, Guru Padmasambhava had entrusted and concealed the actual transmissions of the teachings. In the case of Sa Ter, However, before discovering those transmitted teachings the Tertons first withdraw texts or short coded symbolic scripts from various places, such as rocks, lakes and sky. Then, by seeing or reading them, the Tertons awaken the transmission and discover the true and whole teachings in the essential nature of their minds. Sa Ter (Earth Dharma Treasure) is named thus because the Tertons use those symbolic scripts etc., which are discovered in the earth, as the key for discovering the teachings. Most of the important Sa Ter fall into two major categories.

Firstly, there is the important Ter Cho (gTer Chos) literature which is in three parts: Lama (Bla Ma), Dzogchen (rDzogs Chen) and Thugje Chenpo (Thugs rJe Chen Po).

Bla Ma: The Peaceful and Wrathful Guru Sādhanas:

1 Bla Ma gSang 'Dus	of Guru Chos dBang (1212–1270)
2 Thugs sGrub	of Rig 'Dzin rGod lDem (1337–1408)
3 Bla Ma Nor Bu rGya mTsho	of Padma Gling Pa (1450–?)
4 Thugs sGrub	of Ratna Gling Pa (1403–1478)
5 Guru Drag dMar	of Nyang Nyi Ma 'Od Zer (1124–1193)
6 Guru Drag dMar	of Ratna Gling Pa

rDzogs Chen: The scriptures on rDzogs Chen teachings:

1 Vima sNying Thig	of lDang Ma Lhun rGyal
Its commentary, Bla Ma Yang Tig	by Kun mKhyen Klong Chen Pa (1308–1363)
2 mKha' 'Gro sNying Thig	of Padma Las 'Brel rTsal (1291–1315?)
Its commentary, mKha' 'Gro Yang Tig	by Kun mKhyen Klong Chen Pa
2a Zab Mo Yang Tig, a commentary of both Vima sNying Thig and mKha' 'Gro Yang Tig	by Kun mKhyen Klong Chen Pa
3 dGongs Pa Zang Thal	of Rig 'Dzin rGod lDem
4 Kun bZang dGongs 'Dus	of Padma Gling Pa

Thugs rJe Chen Po: Avalokiteśvara scriptures:

1 Mani bKa' 'Bum	of Grub Thob Ngos Grub and Nyang
2 Yang sNing 'Dus Pa	of Guru Chos dBang
3 bDe gShegs Kun 'Dus	of sMin Gling gTer Chen (1646–1714)

Secondly, there is another important gTer Chos with three parts bKa' brGyad, dGongs 'Dus, and Phur Pa.

bKa' brGyad: There are three major texts:

1 bKa' brGyad bDe bShegs 'Dus Pa (13 vols.)	of mNga' bDag Nyang
2 bKa' brGyad gSang Ba Yongs rDzogs (6 vols.)	of Guru Chos dBang

3 bKa' brGyad Drag Po Rang Byung Rang Shar (4 vol)	of Rig 'Dzin rGod lDem

dGongs 'Dus

1 Bla Ma dGongs 'Dus (13 vol)	of Sangs rGyas Gling Pa (1340–1396)

Phur Pa: (vajrakīla)

1 sPu Gri	of Guru Chos dBang
2 Yang gSang Bla Med	of Ratna Gling Pa

(b) Gong Ter (dGongs gTer). These teachings are discovered directly from the enlightened nature of the minds of the Tertons themselves without using any key such as symbolic script discovered from the earth. So, they are called Gong Ter or Mind Dharma Treasure. Some of the texts of those teachings are:

1 mDzod bDun (the seven treasures)	of Kun mKhyen Klong Chen Pa
2 gNam Chos	of Mi 'Gyur rDo rJe
3 Klong Chen sNying Thig	of Kun mKhyen 'Jigs Med Gling Pa (1729–1798)

(3) Dag Nang (Dag sNang). These are scriptures received from divinities and Gurus by tertons in pure meditative vision.

1 sNying Thig texts	of gYu Thog Yon Tan mGon Po
2 Rig 'Dzin Srog sGrub	of Lha bTsun Nam mKha' 'Jigs Med (1597–1650?)

Collection of Ter Chos and Dag Nang: Kongtrul Yongten Gyatso (Kong sPrul Yon Tan rGya mTsho, 1813–1899) brought together many of the important Ter Chos in a collection of sixty-one volumes called the Rin chen gTer mDzod. It was printed in dPal sPung monastery (Kham), mTshur Phu monastery (central Tibet) and in Delhi, India.

(iv) Study

The main texts for study of the sūtra root texts and commentaries are: the Phar Phyin (Prajñāparamitā), dBu Ma (Madhymaka), 'Dul Ba (Vinaya and mNgon Pa (Abhidharma). The main tantras to be studied are: the Guhyagarbha Tantra with commentaries, the mDzod bDun of

Kunkhyen Longchenpa, sDom gSum (three precepts) of Ngari Panchen (Nga Ris Pan Chen, 1487-1542) and the texts on Kama and Terma by Minling Terchen, and Lochen Dharmaśrī and others.

In the present century the major works on sūtra to be studied are the texts of the gZhung Chen bCu gSum (Thirteen Great Texts) and the commentaries written on them by Patrul Rinpoche (dPal sPrul, 1808–1887) in six volumes, Miphan Namgyal (Mi Pham rNam rGyal, 1846–1912) in thirty-two volumes and especially the commentaries of Zhenphen Choskyi Nangwa (gZhan Phan Chos Kyi sNang Ba). The gZhung Chen bCu gSum (Thirteen Great Texts) are:

1	So Sor Thar Pa'i mDo (Pratimokṣasūtra)	by Śākyamuni Buddha
2	'Dul Ba mDo rTsa Ba (Vinayasūtra)	by Guṇaprabha
3	mNgon Pa Kun bTus (Abidharmasamuccaya)	by Asaṅgha
4	mNgon Pa mDzod (Abhidharmakoṣa)	by Vasubandhu
5	dBu Ma rTsa Ba Shes Rab (Prajñā nāma mūla madhyamaka)	by Nāgārjuna
6	dBu Ma La 'Jug Pa (Madhyamakāvatāra)	by Candrakīrti
7	dBu Ma bZhi brGya Pa (Catuḥśatakaśātra)	by Āryadeva
8	Byang Chub Sems dPa'i sPyod Pa La 'Jug Pa (Bodhicaryāvatrāra)	by Śāntideva
9	Phar Phyin mNgon rTogs rGyan (Abhisamayālamkāra nāma Prajñāpāramitā)	by Asaṅgha
10	Thegs Pa Chen Po'i rGyud Bla Ma'i (Mahāyānasūtrālaṁkāra)	by Asaṅgha
11	dBus mTha' rNam 'Byed (Madhyāntavibhaṅga)	by Asaṅgha
12	Chos Dang Chos Nyid rNam 'Byed (Dharmadharmatāvibhaṅga)	by Asaṅgha
13	Thegs Pa Chen Po'i rGyud Bla Ma'i (Mahāyānottarantantra)	by Asaṅgha

(b) The literature of the Sarma School

The other three major Buddhist schools—Kagyud, Sakya and Gelug—are within the Sarma (gSar Ma, New Tantra) tradition. The Sarma schools have many of the same original texts for study and practice. The differences among them result from different lineages of teaching and different interpretations of the subtle meanings of the scriptures by Tibetan scholars and commentators. Also, some of the schools have their own special teachings transmitted from Indian Siddhas such as the Phyag rGya Chen Po (Mahāmudra) of the Kagyud and the gSung Ngag Lam 'Bras (teaching on the Path and Result) of the Sakya. The teachers who first translated and spread the Sarma literature were the great Tibetan translators, Rinchen Zangpo (958–1051), Drogmi (993–1050), Marpa (1012–1099) and others.

(i) The classification of the Dharma

Three Sūtric Yānas:
- (a) Śrāvakayāna (Hinayāna)
- (b) Pratyekabuddhayāna (Hinayāna)
- (c) Bodhisattvayāna (Mahāyāna)

Four Vajrayānas:
- (a) Kriyāyoga
- (b) Caryāyoga
- (c) Yogatantra
- (d) Anuttarayogatantra
    - (1) Pitṛtantra
    - (2) Maṭrtantra
    - (3) Advitīyatantra

(ii) Major texts for study and practice

The basic texts are the literature from the Canon of the Buddha and the works of great Indian scholars in the Kajur and Tenjur collections. But the numerous commentaries written by both Indian and Tibetan scholars contained slightly different interpretations of the basic works. These differences influenced the development of the various schools in

Tibet, as indicated above. In some of the larger monasteries, different monastic colleges (Grva Tshangs) had their own commentarial texts (Yig Cha) to study, practice and uphold.

Some of the major texts for sūtra study are: Pramāṇasamuccaya of Dignāga, Seven Treatises on Logic by Dharmakīrti, Six Treatises by Nāgārjuna on Madhyamaka, Five Treatises by Maitrinath and Asaṅgha on Mahāyāna Philosophy, Abhidharmasamucaya by Asaṅgha and Abhidharmakoṣa by Vasubandhu on Abhidharma, and the Vinayasūtra by Guṇaprabha on Vinaya.

Some of the root tantras are: Guhyasamāja and Vajrabhairava of the Pitṛtantra: Cakrasaṁvara, Mahāmāyā and Hevajra of the Maṭrtantra; and the Kālacakra and Mañjuśrīmūlatantra of Advitīyatantra.

(iii) The literature of the Kagyud school

The founder of the Kagyud school was the great translator and sage Marpa Chokyi Lodro (1012–1099). He visited India three times and received the tantric teachings from Mahāsiddha Nāropa, Maitrīpa and others. He then transmitted and expounded these doctrines in Tibet. The other renowned scholars and sages in the Kagyud lineage are the great yogi Milarepa (1040–1123), the famous scholar Gampopa (1079–1153), the first Karmapa Tusum Khyenpa, Drikung Jigten Sumgon, Tsagpa Gyare, Situ Tenpa'i Nyinche and Kongtrul Yongten Gyatso.

The basic literature for study is the same as for the general Sarma tradition. The highest philosophical teaching of the Kagyud is the Mahāmudrā (Phyag rGya Chen Po) which is a special teaching of this school. Marpa received this teaching from the Indian Mahāsiddha Maitrīpa. It has two aspects: Sūtric Mahāmudrā and Tantric Mahāmudrā. Another important special teaching of this school is the Six Yogas of Nāropa. These Six Yogas are: Heat Yoga (gTum Mo), Illusory Body (sGyu Ma), Dream (rMi Lam), Clear Light ('Od gSal), Intermediate State (Bar Do) and Consciousness Transference (Pho Ba). The Kagyud school emphasizes the basic practice of all three yānas: the practice of revulsion (Nges 'Byung) from saṃsāra of the Śrāvakyāna, developing the Bodhi-Mind (Byang Sems) of the Mahāyāna, and observing the vows (Dam Tshig) of the Vajrayāna.

Some of the Kagyud works for study are:

1 Songs and biographies of Marpa and Milarepa.
2 Writings of Gampopa (3 vols) and Phagmo Trupa (6 vols)
3 Writings of Karmapas Tusum Khyenpa, Rangchung Dorje and Mikyod Dorje.

4 Writings of Ling Repa, Tsangpa Gyare (1 vol.), Drikung Jigten Gonpo, Drugpa Kunleg, Padma Karpo (14 vols), Wangchug Dorje (1555–1603), Zhamar Khachod Wangpo (Zhva dMar mKha' sPyod dBang Po, 1350–1405), Konchog Yonten, Tsuglag Threngwa (gTshug Lag Phreng Ba, 1454–1556) (9 vols), Situ Chojung (12 vols), and Kongtrul Yonten Gyatsho (90 vols).

(iv) The literature of the Sakya school

Khon Konchog Gyalpo founded the Sakya school and built the Sakya monastery in AD 1073. The great scholar and translator Drogmi Yeshe, after studying for many years at Nalanda Mahavihara and other places in India, received many teachings from Siddha Śāntipa, Nāropa, Guhyagarbha and others, and translated them into Tibetan. Drogmi also translated the scriptures of gSung Ngag Lam 'Bras (the teachings of the Path and Result) which he received from Gayadhara and transmitted them to his disciple Khon Konchong Gyalpo. There were five famous scholars of this school known as the Five Supremes (Gong Ma rNam lNga). They were: Sachen Kunga Nyingpo, Sodnam Tsemo, Tragpa Gyaltshen, Sakya Pandita Kunga Gyaltshen and Drogon Chogyal Phagpa. Some of the other great Sakya scholars were: Rongton Shecha Kunrig, Ngorchen Kunga Zangpo, Yagthrug Sangye Pal (1348–?), and Go Rabjam Sodnam Senge.

The main texts for study are those for the Sarma tradition. The major texts for sūtra study are the Six Great Volumes (Pod Chen Drug). They are: Tshad Ma Rig gTer by Sakya Paṇḍita and Pramāṇavārttika by Dharmarkīrti on logic, Vinayasūtra by Guṇaprabha, Abhidharmakoṣa by Vasubandhu, Abhisamayālaṁkāra nāma prajñāpāramitā of Asaṅgha, Madhyamakāvatāra by Candrakīrti and the general texts for sūtra and tantra.

The special teachings of this school are: the teaching of the Path and Result and the Thirteen Golden Doctrines. The Teaching of the Path and Result (gSung Ngag Lam 'Bras) has both sūtric and tantric aspects for realizing the indivisibility of saṃsāra and nirvāṇa('Khor 'Das dByer Med). The Thirteen Golden Doctrines are: Three Doctrines of Ka' 'Pyod Ma, Three Doctrines of dMar Chen divinities, Three Doctrines of dMar Chung divinities and the doctrines of Seng gDong sNgon Mo, 'Jam dPal Nag Po, Chi Med rDo rJe Lha Mo and Jambhala dMar Po.

Some of the Sakya literary works are:

1 The Writings of The Five Supreme Teachers (15 vols).

2 The Works of Ngorchen Kunga Zangpo (4 vols).

3 The Works of Go Rabjam Sodnam Senge (15 vols).
4 The Works of Jamyang Khyentse Wangpo ('JamdByangs mKhyen brTse'i dBang Po, 1820–1892) (10 vols).

(v) The literature of the Gelug school

The eminent scholar Je Tsongkhapa Lobzang Tragpa is the founder of the Gelug school. This lineage is in the tradition of the Kadam school of Atīśa Dīpaṁkāraśrījñāna of India. Je Tsongkhapa expounded and wrote renowned texts and commentaries on sūtras, śastras and tantras, and founded the Gaden monastery in 1409. Some of the numerous scholars and writers of this school are: Khetrub Geleg Palzang, Gyaltshab Darma Rinchen, the 1st Dalai Lama Geduntrub, Jamyang Choje, Jamchen Choje, Sherab Senge, Kunga Tontrub, Panchen Chokyi Gyaltshen, Gyalwang Sodnam Gyatsho (rGyal dBang bSod Nams rGya mTsho, 1617–1682), and Jamyang Zhepa Ngawang Tsondru.

The texts for study are the same as mentioned for Sarma. Their main emphasis for study and practice are: the strict observance of monastic discipline, the study of the texts through reasoning of logical expression, adherence to the philosophical doctrine of Prāsaṅgika Madhyamaka, practice of Dharma in the system of 'Three Stages of the Path' and accomplishing the innate wisdom (lHan sKyes Kyi Ye Shes) and Illusory-Body (sGyu Lus) through the practice of two stages (Rim gNyis) of Guhyasamāja, Cakrasaṁvara, Vajrabhairava, Kālacakra and other tantras.

Some of the enormous literary works of Gelug scholars are:

1 The works of Je Tsong Khapa (20 vols, 210 treatises).
2 The works of Khetrub Geleg Palzang (10 vols).
3 The works of Gyaltshab Darma Rinchen (8 vols).
4 The works of Duldzin Tragpa Gyaltshen ('Dul 'Dzin Grags Pa rGyal mTshan, 1374–?) (2 vols).
5 The works of Panchen Gedentrub (5 vols).
6 The works of Panchen Sodtrag (bSod Grags).
7 The works of Jetsun Chokyi Gyaltshen.
8 The works of Panchen Lozang Chokyi Gyaltsen (5 vols).
9 The works of Gyalwang Ngapa (rGyal dBang lNga Pa) (30 vols).
10 The works of Changkya Rolpa'i Dorje (lCang sKya Rol Pa'i rDo rJe, 1717–?) (5 vols).

11 The works of Jamyang Zhepa (15 vols).
12 The works of Longdol Lama (Klong rDol, 1719–1794).

(vi) The literature of some minor schools

(1) Zhi Ched—a great siddha of India, Phadampa Sangye, visited Tibet five times (last time in AD 1098) and taught the Zhi Ched (Pacifier of Suffering), the teachings of Transcendental Wisdom (Prajñāparamitā). His tradition is known as Zhi Ched in which the most famous yoginī of Tibet, Machig Labdron, taught the Prajñāpāramitā through practice of Chod (gCod), terminating the defilements. There are many Chod texts of both Kama and Terma traditions and they are practiced in both Kagyud and Nyingma schools.

(2) Jonang—Kunpang Thugje Tsondru (1243–?) founded a monastery at a place called Jonang and his tradition is known as the Jonang. In this tradition both Kunkhyen Dolpo Sherab Gyaltshen (1292–1361), a great scholar (especially of Kālacakratantra) and the well-known historian Tārānāth (1575–?) wrote many famous literary works on various subjects.

(3) Shangpa Kagyud—the Great Siddha, Khyungpo Naljor, received the teachings of Six Yogas of Niguma and Five Tantras from Niguma, Maitrīpa and Sukhasiddhi in India and he taught them in Tibet.

(4) Zhalu (Zhva Lu—the celebrated Tibetan scholar Puton Rinchenrub (Bu sTon Rin Chen Grub, 1290–1364)) became a great master of Kālacakratana and seventy other doctrines. He edited and put into present form the Kajur and Tenjur collections. His tradition is also known as Pulug (Bu Lugs).

(5) Podong—Podong Chogle Namgyal (Bo Dong Phyogs Las rNam rGyal, 1375–1451), who was a great scholar and writer, founded this tradition. He wrote 132 volumes of texts and commentaries on various subjects.

Most of the minor schools functioned as distinctive schools when their teachers were living, but at present many of them have merged into one of the major schools, or are a sub-school of one of the major schools. Although they have not retained their identity as separate schools, the works of their great scholars are still studied.

B RELIGIOUS LITERATURE—ACCORDING TO SUBJECT

The religious literature of Tibet can be divided into four categories: religion; history and biography; poetic composition and yogic songs; and music, dance, art and architecture. Religion comprises the main body of the literature and the other categories are branches of it.

1 Religion

There are various ways of arranging this vast body of literature but all of its works fall into three categories: the View, the Practice and the Conduct.

Some of the texts on View (lTa Ba, Darsan, Skt.) are:

1 Hinayāna:	Abhidharmakoṣa	by Vasubandhu
2 Mahāyāna:	Six Treatises on Madhyamaka	by Nāgārjuna
3 Vajrayāna:	Man Ngag lTa 'Phreng	by Padmasambhava

Some of the texts on Practice (bsGom Pa) are:

1 Sūtra:	Bodhipathapradīpa	by Dīpaṁkaraśrījñāna
2 Tantra:	sNgags Rim Chen Mo	by Je Tsongkhapa

Some of the texts on Conduct (sPyod Pa) are:

1 Pratimokṣa:	Vinayasūtra	by Guṇaprabha
2 Bodhisattva:	Bodhicaryāvatāra	by Śāntideva
3 Tantra:	sNgags sDom from sDom gSum rNam Nges	by Dharmaśrī

2 History and biography

The Chojung (Chos 'Byung, religious history) works recount the major events in the transmission of the teaching and the activities of the teachers and their disciples. Some of the major Chojung texts are:

1 Ma Ni bKa' 'Bum	by Trubthob Ngotrub and Nyang
2 Padma bKa' Thang	by Orgyan Lingpa
3 Thub bsTan gSal Bar Byed Pa'i Nyi 'Od	by Longchen Rabjam

4	Chos 'Byung Rin Po Che'i mDzod	by Buton
5	Sa sKya'i gDung Rabs	by Kunga Sodnam
6	Padma rGyas Pa'i Nyin Byed	by Padma Karpo
7	mKhas Pa'i dGa' sTon	by Tshuglag Threngwa
8	dGos 'Dod Kun 'Byung	by Tārānātha
9	Ba'i Dur Ser Po	by Sangya Gyatsho (1653–1705)
10	'Dzam Gling Tha Gru Khyab Pa'i rGyan	by Jigme Lingpa
11	Lha dBang gYul Las rGyal Ba'i rNga Bo Che'i sGra dByang	by Jigtral Yeshe Dorje

Some of the rNam Thar (Biography) texts are: Padma bKa' Thang—the biography of Padmasambhava, Vai Ro'i 'Dra 'Bag, and biographies of Jowo Atīśa, Marpa, Milarepa, Sakya Paṇḍita, Chogyal Phagpa, Longchen Rabjam, Je Tsongkhapa, rGyal dBang lNga Pa and Ngos Kyi Yul Dang Ngos Kyi Mi Mang of the 14th Dalai Lama.

3 Poetic composition and yogic songs

There are two major aspects of Tibetan religious poetry: poems (sNyan Ngag) and yogic songs (mGur).

The religious poems in the Tenjur are:

1	Bodhisattvāvadāna Kalpalatā	by Kṣemendra
2	Buddhacarita	by Aśvaghoṣa
3	Jatakamala	by Āryaśūra

Some of the Tibetan works are: the poetic literature written by Karmapa Mikyod Dorje, Tārānātha, Pawo Tsuglag Threngwa, Gyalwang Ngapa Chenpo (the Great 5th Dalai Lama), Minling Lochen Gungthang Tentron, Do Kharwa, and Mipham Namgyal.

Some of the yogic songs are:

1	Dohākoṣagīti	by Saraha
2	Dohās of other Mahāsiddhas	from the Tenjur
3	mGur 'Bum	of Milarepa

4	bKa' rGyud mGur mTsho	of Mikyod Dorje
5	mGur 'Bum	of Drugpa Kunleg
6	mGur	of Changkya Rolpa'i Dorje
7	mGur	of Lhatsun Namkha Jigme
8	mGur 'Bum	of Zhabs dKar Ba (1781–1850)

4 Music, dance, art and architecture

Music and dance—In the sūtric tradition, musical instruments (Rol Mo or Rol Cha) and vocal music (dByang), are used to accompany religious ceremonies, but in the tantra they are an important part of the practice itself. Sacred dances are also performed in order to transform oneself into the divinity and to show this aspect to others. There are many texts on the performance of music (dByang Yig) and dance ('Cham Yig) and their significance.

Art and architecture—In the vinaya and tantric texts there is a body of literature which is comprised of manuals of instructions for the architecture of temples, monastic residences and stūpas. There is also an extensive literature that gives detailed instructions for the proper proportions and design of Maṇḍalas (the structures of Buddha-fields), Cakras (mystic diagrams) and Images.

2

THE SECULAR LITERATURE

Except for some texts in the Tenjur collection, there is little Tibetan literature that was not influenced by religious conceptions. The Tenjur texts whose subject matter is predominantly secular are: 67 treatises (21 vols) on logic; 28 treatises (2 vols) on grammar; 7 treatises (5 vols) on medicine; 18 treatises (½ vol.) on art; and 57 treatises (7½ vols) on other general subjects.

On the basis of subject matter, there are a number of other important Tibetan literary works which are considered within the secular literature. They are included under the following headings: history; grammar; poetic composition; metrical literature and lexicons; logic; astrology; mathematics; medicine; geography and cosmology; law; political writings; music and dance; drama; and arts and crafts.

1 HISTORY (rGyal Rabs)

In Tibetan literature there are two major aspects of history (Lo rGyus): secular history (rGyal Rabs) and religious history (Chos 'Byung). The secular history mainly relates the events in the succession of kings and other political and social happenings. There are works dealing with both the older period of Tibetan history and works concerned with more recent times.

Some major works of historical literature are:

1 bKa' Chen Ka Khol Ma	Will of King Srongtsan Gampo
2 rBa bZhed Zhabs bTags Ma	by Ba Salnang and Ba Sangshi
3 rBa bZhed gTsang Ma	by Ba Salnang and Ba Sangshi
4 Deb Ther dMar Po (1346)	by Tshalpa Kunga Dorje

5	rGyal Po, Blon Po and bTsun Mo bKa' Thang	by Ogyen Lingpa (Terma)
6	Deb ther dMar Po (gSar Pa)	by Sodnam Tragpa
7	Deb Ther sNgon Po	by Golo Zhonu Pal
8	Bod Kyi rGyal Rabs from mKhas Pa'i dGa' sTon	by Tsuglag Threngwa
9	Bod Kyi rGyal Rabs gSal Ba'i Me Long	by Sakya Sodnam Gyaltshen
10	Bod Kyi Deb Ther dPyid Kyi rGyal Mo'i Glu dByangs	by 5th Dalai Lama
11	Deb Ther rGya mTsho	by Tragon Zhabtrung (1801–?)
12	Deb Ther dKar Po	by Gedun Chophel (1905–1951)
13	Bod Kyi Srid Don rGyal Rabs	by W.D. Shakabpa (1907–)

2 GRAMMAR

Tibetan grammatical literature contains both texts and commentaries on Sanskrit grammar translated from Indian sources and grammatical texts for the Tibetan language itself. It was important for scholars to know Sanskrit grammar because so much literature was translated from Sanskrit into Tibetan and the Tibetan alphabet, grammar, and literary forms were formed on the basis of Sanskrit models.

Some of the important Sanskrit grammar texts translated into Tibetan are:

1	Pāṇini vyākaraṇasūtra	by Pāṇini
2	Candra vyākaraṇasūtra	by Candragomin
3	Kalāpa vyākaraṇasūtra	by Saptavarman
4	Sārasvata vyākaraṇa	by Anubhūti

In addition to the commentaries on Sanskrit grammars by Indian scholars which are in the Tenjur collection, there are also many commentaries by Tibetan scholars. Commentaries on the Candra vyākaraṇa were written by Lochen Thugje Pal, Zhalu Chokyong Zangpo and Situ Chojung. Panglo wrote a commentary on the Kalāpa and Tārānāth wrote on the Sārasvata.

Some of the Tibetan grammar texts are:

1	Lung sTon Pa Sum Cu Pa	by Thonmi Sambhota

2 rTags Kyi 'Jug Pa	by Thonmi Sambhota
3 sMa Ba'i sGo mTshen Cha	by Drenpa'i Yeshe
4 gNas brGyad Chen Po'i rTsa Ba	by lCe Khyi 'Brug

The first two texts, Sum Cu Pa and rTags 'Jug, are root grammar texts for the Tibetan language. There are many works on these two texts and some of them are:

1 Sum rTags 'Grel Ba	by Narthang Lotsawa
2 Sum rTags 'Grel Ba	by Zhalu Lotsawa Chokyong Zangpo (1441–?)
3 Sum rTags 'Grel Ba	by Panchen Sodnam Namgyal
4 Sum rTags 'Grel Ba	by Lochen Namkha Zangpo (1400–?)
5 Sum rTags 'Grel Ba	by Othrungpa Karma Rabgye
6 Sum rTags 'Grel Ba	by Zurkhar Lotro Gyatsho
7 Sum rTags 'Grel Ba	by Pawo Tsuglag Threngwa
8 Sum rTags 'Grel Ba	by Drati Geshe Rinchen Dontrub
9 Sum rTags 'Grel Chen mKhas Pa'i mGul rGyan Mu Tig 'Phreng mDzes	by Situ Chokyi Nangwa

3 POETIC COMPOSITION, METRICAL LITERATURE AND LEXICONS

(a) Poetic literature

There is a vast poetic literature in the Tibetan language. There are also a number of works that deal with the rules and system of ancient Indian poetry. Especially important are the Kāvyādarśa by Daṇḍin and the Meghadūta by Kālidāsa.

Some of the well-known Tibetan commentaries on Kāvyādarśa are written by: Panglo Jamyang Khache, Rinpungpa, Pawo, 5th Dalai Lama, Podkhepa, Minling Lochen, Khampa Chokyi Nyima, Mipham Namgyal and Ogyen Kunzang Tendzin.

Some of the great Tibetan poems are contained in the works of: Sakya Paṇḍita, Kunkhyen Longchenpa, Je Tsongkhapa, Karmapa Mikyod Dorje, 5th Dalai Lama, Dokharpa and Kunkhyen Jigme Lingpa.

(b) Metrical literature

The major text for metre (sDeb sByor) is the Chandoratnākara by Ratnākaraśāntipāda. Some of the important Tibetan works on metre are the commentaries written by Mikyod Dorje, Minling Lochen and Gyurme Tendzin.

(c) Lexicons

The principal lexicon texts (mNgon brJod) are: the bilingual (Tibetan-Sanskrit) lexicon Bye Brag Tu rTogs Par Byed Pa by Tibetan scholars; the Amarakoṣa ('Chi Med mDzod) by Amarsiṁha and its commentary. Kāmadhenu ('Dod 'Jo'i Ba); Abhidhānamuktāmālā (mNgon brJod Mu Tig Phreng Ba) by Śrīdharasena. The last three works are translated from Sanskrit. The important Tibetan works are: mNgon brJod Tshig Gi gTer by Sakya Paṇḍita and Prajñā (Shes Rab) by Sakyapa Tendzin Gyaltshen.

4 LOGIC

There are a large number of texts on logic written by both Indian and Tibetan logicians. The famous works of Buddhist logic such as those of Dignāga and Dharmakīrti were written in order to refute non-Buddhist philosophies and to defend Buddhist teachings. The method of argument was based upon logical reasoning rather than an appeal to scripture or faith. Logic is classified as a common or secular subject by Buddhist scholars, including Dignāga, and the works of this subject are not regarded as religious scriptures.

Some of the principal Indian works are:

1	Pramanasamuccaya	by Dignāga
2	Pramāṇavārttika Kārikā etc. the Seven Treatises	by Dharmakīrti
3	Tattvasaṁgraha Kārikā	by Śāntarakṣita

Some of the main Tibetan works are:

1	Tshad Ma bsDus Pa Yid Kyi Mun Sel	by Cha(Phyva)pa Choseng
2	Tshad Ma Rig gTer	by Sakya Paṇḍita

3 Tshad Ma Rig sNang	by Bodong Chogle Namgyal (1375/6–1451)

Some of the major commentaries on logical texts written by Tibetan authors are the works of Gyaltshab Je, Rongton, Go Rabjampa and Mipham Namgyal.

5 ASTROLOGY

The major text for Tibetan astrology is the Kālacakratantra (in the Kajur collection) and its famous commentaries. The Lalitavistara and dPal mKha' 'Gro rGya mTsho (Śrī ḍākārṇava) tantra in the Kajur also contain some material on astrology. The calendar of sixty-year cycles (Rab Byung) was introduced in Tibet in AD 1027 as a result of the introduction of the Kālacakratantra. The eminent scholars Buton (1290–1364) and Dolpo (1292–?) wrote many treatises on the Kālacakratantra. In later centuries four main traditions of astrology developed:

(a) Phug Lugs (tradition of Phug Pa). This is the tradition of those who followed the astrological texts of Pad dKar Zhal Lung and the supplementary texts written by Norzang Gyatsho (1423–1513) and Phugpa Lhuntrub Gyatsho.

(b) mTshur Lugs (tradition of mTshur). The tradition of the followers of the astrological literature written by Tshurphu Dontrub Odzer.

(c) Phug Lugs Grub rTsis. This is a later astrological tradition based on the texts Ba'i Dur dKar Po by Desrid Sangye Gyatsho and the Nyin Byed sNang Ba by Minling Lochen.

(d) mTshur Lugs Grub sTsis. This tradition is based on the text Nyer mKho Bum bZang by Ngeleg Tendzin.

Some of the other important texts written by Tibetan astrologers are:

1 rTsis Kyi bsTan Chos mKhas Pa dGa' Byed	by Buton
2 lNga bDus Lag Len and others	by Dolpho
3 Dus 'Khor 'Grel Chen	by Khetrub Je
4 rTsis Kun bsDus Pa	by Rangjung Dorje
5 Pad dKar Zhal Lung	by Norzang Gyatsho
6 Dus 'Khor 'Grel Chen and others	by Mipham Namgyal

7 rTsis gZhung Rig lDan sNying Thig — by Khyenrab Norbu (1890–1962)

6 MATHEMATICS

As mathematics is an elementary and essential part of astrology the traditional source of mathematics has been the commentaries on the Kālacakratantra. The Abhidharmakoṣa and Lalitavistara also contain some material on numerical systems. Some of the Tibetan texts on numerical systems are:

1 rDel-rTsis rTsa-Ba Leu brGyad-Pa — by Ananda
2 Khun-Phan Me-Long — by bTsan-sPro-Ba
3 'Phrul-Yig lDe-Mig — by Ngag-dBang Ch'os-'Byor

But there are no modern mathematical texts. It is important to develop such texts in order for Tibetan-speaking people to keep abreast of educational developments.

7 MEDICINE

There were some Indian and a large number of Tibetan works in the field of medicine. There are also some methods of medical treatment in the vinaya sūtras. The other major Indian medical texts translated into Tibetan are the Aṣṭāngahṛdaya saṁhitā by Vāgbhaṭa and the Yogaśataka by Nāgārjuna.

The greatest Tibetan physician was the later Yuthog Yontan Gonpo (gYu Thog Yon Tan mGon Po) who lived in the twelfth century. (There was another great Tibetan physician by the name of Yuthog who lived in the ninth century.)

The main textual source for Tibetan medicine is the sMan Gyi rGyud bZhi (the Four Tantras of Medicine). The Four Tantras are: rTsa rGyud; bShad rGyud; Man Ngag rGyud; and rGyud Phyi Ma. The authorship of the Four Tantras is disputed but they are generally believed to be canons translated by Vairocana from Sanskrit into Tibetan and then concealed as Hidden Treasures at Samye Monastery. In the eleventh century, the great Terton Traba Ngonshechen (Grva Ba mNgon Shes Can, 1012–1090) discovered and transmitted them to the later Yuthog Yonten Gonpo. Yuthog practiced and taught the Four Tantras and wrote about twenty treatises on them and other aspects of medicine. The two major traditions which developed from this lineage are (a) Byang Pa and (b) Zur.

(a) Byang Pa. The tradition was founded by Changpa Rigden (Byang Pa Rig lDan) and his followers who wrote many treatises on medicine.

(b) Zur.This tradition was established by the great physician Zurkhar Nyamnyid Dorje (Zur mKhar mNyam Nyid rDo rJe) who edited the Four Tantras. He and his followers wrote extensively on medical subjects.

Desrid Sangye Gyatsho wrote the famous Ba'i Dur sNgon Po and other texts. He also founded a medical college at Lhasa.

Some of the other medical texts are:

1	sMan gZhung Cha Lag bCo brGyad	by Yuthog Yonten Gonpo
2	Treatises on Tantra	by Changpa Rigden Chenpo
3	Bye Ba Ring bSrel	by Zur Nyamnyid Dorje
4	Mes Po'i Zhal Lung	by Zur Khar Lotro Gyatsho (1508–?)
5	gCes bDus	by Drigung
6	bKa' rGya Ma	by Darmo Menrampa
7	Ba'i Dur sNgon Po and Lhan Thabs	by Desrid Sangye Gyatsho

8 GEOGRAPHY AND COSMOLOGY

The traditional Tibetan geographical and cosmological texts are contained within religious works. There is no separate literature for them. The texts in which these subjects are discussed are: the Kālacakratantra (first chapter); 'Jigs rTen gZhag Pa from the Kajur; Abhidharmakoṣa by Vasubandu (third chapter); Yid bZhin Rin Po Che'i mDzod by Kunkhyen Longchenpa; and the various commentaries on these works.

A later work on the geography of Tibet is the 'Jam Gling rGyas bShad by Tsenpo Lama.

9 LAW

The judicial and common law of Tibet was developed by King Srongtsen Gampo in the seventh century. The judicial law was enlarged under King Phagmo Trupa. Until recently these were the only written laws of the state. On 10 March 1963, His Holiness the 14th Dalai Lama promulgated a new constitution.

The literature of the laws of the state are:

(a) Common law—

1 Lha Chos dGe Ba bCu (the 10 virtuous or religious laws)	by King Srongsten Gampo
2 Mi Chos gTsang Ma bCu Drug (the 16 pure or social laws)	by King Srongsten Gampo

(b) Judicial law—

1 Khrims Yig Zhal lCe bCu gSum (the legal text of 13 codes of judicial judgements)	by King Srongsten Gampo
2 Khrims Yig Zhal lCe bCo lNga Pa (the legal text of 15 codes of judgements)	by King Phagmo Trupa (14th century)

(c) New constitution—

1 The Constitution of Tibet	promulgated by the 14th Dalai Lama in 1963

10 POLITICAL WRITINGS

Some of the Indian works are:

1 Prajñāśataka	by Nāgārjuna
2 Nitiśāstra prajñādaṇḍa	by Nāgārjuna
3 Rājaparikathāratna vali (fourth chapter)	by Nāgārjuna
4 Nītiśāstra jantupoṣaṇ bindu	by Nāgārjuna

5 Gathakoṣa	by Ravigupta
6 Śatagāthā	by Vararuci
7 Vimalapraśnottara ratnamālā	by Amoghavarma
8 Cāṇakya rājanītiśāstra	by Cāṇakya
9 Nītiśāstra	by Masūrākṣa

Some of the Tibetan works are:

1 Legs Par bShad Pa Rin Po Che'i gTer	by Sakya Paṇḍita
2 Lugs gNyis Kyi bSlab Bya Mu Thu Li 'Phreng Ba	by the 5th Dalai Lama
3 rGyal Po Lugs Kyi bsTan bCos Sa gZhi sKong Ba'i rGyan	by Mipham Namgyal

11 MUSIC AND DANCE

There are different traditions of Tibetan vocal (Glu dByangs) and Instrumental (Rol Cha) music. A great many writings exist on the notation of religious chant (dByangs-Yig) and religious musical instruments (Rol-Tshig or Nga-Tshig). However, most of this music was orally communicated from generation to generation. There is probably little written on secular music. Now it is important that it be preserved in writing and on records for the benefit of future generations.

12 DRAMA

Two dramatic works from the Tenjur are listed below as well as some native Tibetan dramas. As with music and dance, it is important to translate this dramatic literature into contemporary dramatic forms and to expand it with new works.

From the Tenjur:

1 Lokanandanataka	by Candragomin
2 Nāgānanda nāma nāṭaka	by Harśadeva

Some Tibetan works are:

1 gZugs Kyi Nyi Ma
2 Dri Med Kun lDan
3 'Gro Ba bZang Mo
4 Pad Ma'i Tshal Gyi Zlos Gar by Patrul Rinpoche

13 ARTS AND CRAFTS

There are many craft traditions in Tibet such as drawing, painting, writing, weaving, stitching, sculpture, metalwork, carpentry and construction. There are some texts of instructions such as the bZo'i Pa Khra by Mipham Namgyal, but they are mostly taught through oral and practical demonstration.

Tibetan literature is a vast accumulation of works written over thirteen centuries by authors who addressed themselves to an encyclopedic range of subjects. While it is impossible to cover this entire body of literature, I have tried to impart its general structure for English-speaking readers who are interested in expanding their knowledge of Tibetan culture.

Glossary of Buddhist terms

Abhidharma One of the three collections (Tripitaka) of Buddhist canonical writings. It sets forth the teachings of the Buddha on metaphysics.

Absolute Truth (Paramārtha, Skt.) See Two Truths.

Ācārya A spiritual master.

Arhat One who has subdued emotional defilement. The fourth and final attainment of the Śrāvakayāna. 'Foe-Subduer' is the traditional Tibetan meaning for this term. 'Worthy One' is the common Theravadin meaning.

Bhikṣu A fully ordained Buddhist monk who observes the 254 rules of conduct.

Bodhicitta Mind of Enlightenment; an attitude intentionally directed toward benefiting all sentient beings.

Bodhipākṣika Dharma
The thirty-seven Wings of Enlightenment:

(1) 4 Smṛtyupasthāna—four Foundations of Mindfulness
(2) 4 Samyakprahana—four Efforts
(3) 4 Ṛddhipāda—four Types of Powers
(4) 5 Indriya —five Faculties or Controlling Powers
(5) 5 Bala—five Forces
(6) 7 Bodhyaṅga—seven Elements of Enlightenment
(7) Arya-Aṣṭrāngāmarga—eightfold Noble Path.

These are the thirty-seven essential aspects of the Buddhist path of practice. The first twelve are for the practice of the Path of Accumulation, the next ten are for the Path of Application, the next seven are for the Path of Insight and the final eight are for the Path of Meditation.

Bon (Tib.) The native religion of Tibet before the advent of Buddhism.

Buddha A fully Enlightened Being.

Cakra Energy centers within the human body, the understanding and control of which constitute an essential part of the esoteric path of Buddhism. In the esoteric teachings of Buddhism there are systems of three, four and five cakras or more.

Chod (gCod, Tib.) Cutting off the ego. A special practice based on the Prajñāpāramitā texts. It was taught by Phadampa and then by Machig Labdron for cutting through attachment to phenomena and self.

Chogyal (Chos rGyal, Tib.) Dharma King. This is also the name of the dynasty of the earliest rulers of Tibet (second century BC to tenth century AD).

Dharma Buddhism, or the Buddhist scriptures, practices and attainments.

Dharmakāya The Absolute Body of the Enlightened One. This aspect of the Buddha is represented symbolically in the Nyingma Tradition as Samantabhadra, the Primordial Buddha (Adibuddha) who resides in a condition free from all elaboration.

Dharma Nairātmya The non-substantive nature of phenomena, realization of which is synonymous with the realization of Śūnyatā (Skt., voidness) of phenomena. It is the special realization of the Bodhisattva path. By contrast, the Arhat realizes only the non-substantive nature of the human personality (Pudgala Nairātmya, Skt.).

Dharmapāla Spiritual forces which protect and preserve the Dharma.

Dzog Rim (Tib.) (Sampannakrama, Skt.) The Completion Stage. A method of tantric meditation in which one attains bliss, clarity and no-thought through the means of the channels (rTsa, Tib.), energy flow (rLung, Tib.) and essence (Thig Le, Tib.) within the human body.

Also a method of spiritual attainment by means of meditation on the Tsa, Lung and Thig Le which dissolves all phenomena into the meditative state.

Eighty-four Mahāsiddha A group of famous Indian Buddhist adepts of meditation traditionally noted for their esoteric attainments.

Five Certainties The certainties of teachers, disciples, teachings, time and place.

Four Truths

(1) The truth of suffering.
(2) The truth of the origin of suffering.
(3) The truth of the cessation of suffering.
(4) The truth of the path to the cessation of suffering.

The Four Truths cover the whole of the Buddhist teachings. The

Four Noble Truths were the first teaching which the Lord Buddha delivered in his sermon given at the Deer Park near Vārāṇasī.

Four Paths

(1) Sambhāramārga—path of accumulation.
(2) Prayogamārga—path of application.
(3) Darśanamārga—path of insight.
(4) Bhāvanāmārga—path of meditation.

These are the stages of the practice through which a Buddhist practitioner attains the goal of Buddhahood.

Four Stages of Result

(1) Stream-Enterer.
(2) Once-Returner.
(3) Never-Returner.
(4) Arhat.

These stages refer to the four degrees of spiritual maturation according to the Hinayana tradition: (1) having merely entered the 'stream' of the Buddhist teachings, (2) having progressed to the point that one will only be reborn in samsara one more time, (3) never having to be reborn in samsara, and (4) having achieved a final victory over the defiling forces (Kleśas, Skt.) of samsaric existence.

Guru Source of spiritual guidance and teaching. See ***Lama***.

Hearing Transmission See Transmission.

Hearing Transmission See ***Transmission.***

Path (Mahāyāna, Skt.), it does not stress the cultivation of the Mind of Enlightenment (Bodhicitta, Skt.). Nowadays the followers of this path are known as Theravadins (The Elders).

Indication Transmission See ***Transmissions.***

Insight Meditation (Vipaśyanā, Skt.) Meditation whose purpose is the progressive realization of the essentially empty nature of all phenomena.

Kajur (bKa' 'Gyur, Tib.) The collection of canonical writings of the Buddha translated into Tibetan. It was assembled by Buton (1290–1364) in 108 volumes.

Karma The process of cause and effect. The inexorable fact of retribution: that every action of body, speech or mind has a definite result though perhaps delayed and subtle. Contemplation of this truth is conducive to spiritual maturation.

Karuna Strong compassion toward sentient beings, perceiving their suffering along with the ardent wish that they may be free from suffering.

Kleśa Emotional defilements.

Kyed Rim (bsKyed Rim, Tib.) The Developing Stage of meditative practices which involve the visualization and contemplation of Enlightened Awareness in the form of deities for the ultimate purpose of realizing the essential purity of all phenomena.

Lam Dre (Lam 'Bras). The Holy Words of Path and Result. The highest esoteric teachings of the Sakya school, traditionally associated with the Mahāsiddha Virūpa.

Lama (Bla Ma, Tib.) The highest one, a spiritual master or teacher.

Lung (rLung, Tib) The subtle energy flow within the channels (rTsa) of the human body. The understanding and control of this flow constitutes part of the training in esoteric Buddhist teachings.

Madhyamaka The Middle Way. One of the major Buddhist philosophical schools whose primary tenets were propagated by Nāgārjuna and Āryadeva. Through its methods all philosophical views are shown to be vacuous, thereby helping to establish the central notion of this school—that all phenomena are inherently void (Śūnyatā).

Mahāmudrā (The Great Seal) The highest and main esoteric practices of the Kagyud school of Tibetan Buddhism.

Mahāpararinirvāṇa The Great Cessation or Transcendence of Sorrow, also refers to the physical death of Śākyamuni Buddha.

Mahāyāna The Greater Vehicle, because it stresses the great importance of cultivating the Mind of Enlightenment (Bodhicitta). Along with others, the Tibetan Buddhists are followers of the Mahāyāna.

Maitri (Loving-Kindness) The strong wish that all sentient beings may have happiness. This is one of the Four Immeasurables (Aprameda, Skt.); so-called because there is no limit to this attitude.

Maṇḍala An assemblage of many things or the structure of a Buddha-field. In Tantric Buddhism this often refers to the circular assemblage of deities, their retinues, and the pure land in which they dwell.

Mantra (sNgags, Tib.) Sacred syllables which invoke or express the essential nature of deities. These are used as a medium to receive esoteric transmission.

Mantrayāna Esoteric teachings. This term refers especially to esoteric practice with mystic syllables.

Māyā Body Illusory Body. Through certain esoteric practices the meditator comes to see all phenomena as the mandalas of the tantric deities, which appear like an illusory body.

Milk Ocean (Dhanakoṣa, Skt.) The milky-white lake from which Guru Rinpoche (Padmasambhava) was miraculously born.

Mind-Transmission See *Transmission.*

Nalanda University An ancient and great seat of Buddhist learning in northern India, now in the state of Bihar. Nāgārjuna was one of its many famous scholars. Nāropa was one of its abbots. Both exoteric and esoteric studies were taught there.

Nirmāṇakāya The form-body of Buddha which is visible to ordinary people. See *Tulku.*

No-Thought Mind free from conceptualization. Through tantric practice one achieves a wisdom which has the qualities of uninterrupted bliss, clarity and no-thought.

Pāramitā The six perfections:

(1) Dāna—generosity
(2) Śīla—moral conduct
(3) Kṣānti—patience
(4) Vīrya—perseverance
(5) Samādhi—contemplation
(6) Prajña—wisdom

These perfections are practiced by Bodhisattvas for the benefit of all sentient beings.

Prajñā Discriminating Insight. This term includes three kinds of wisdom:

(1) The wisdom of hearing.
(2) The wisdom of pondering.
(3) The wisdom of meditation.

This is the wisdom which has the insight that all phenomena have the absolute nature of Śūnyatā.

Prāsaṅgika Madhyamaka A school of the Madhyamaka doctrine of Nāgārjuna, interpreted by Buddhapālita and Candrakīrti, which uses the philosophical techniques of forcing the advocates of opposing views to the absurd limits implied by their assertions.

Pratimokṣa Vows regarding conduct conducive to spiritual maturation, of which there are eight types:

(1) Precepts kept on lunar observance days (Upāvasatha).
(2) Precepts for laymen (Upāsakā).
(3) Precepts for Laywomen (Upāsikā).
(4) Precepts for novice monks (Śrāmaṇera).

(5) Precepts for novice nuns (Śrāmaṇerikā).
(6) Training precepts for women probationers (Śīkśāmaṇa).
(7) For monks (Bhikṣu).
(8) For nuns (Bhikṣunī).

Pratītyasamutpāda Interdependent Arising. The fact that no facet of experience is isolated, singular, self-sufficient, or due to a single causal factor. Everything arises due to and owes its existence to a multitude of interdependently working factors.

Pudgala Nairātmya The realizations of the stage of Arhat, that the human personality is non-substantive and empty in nature.

Pure Land The naturally resplendent lands in which completely Enlightened Buddhas continuously teach for the benefit of all sentient beings. There are two kinds of pure lands:

Manifested Pure Lands.

Pure Lands with Five Certainties.

Relative Truth (Saṁvṛiti Satya, Skt.) See *Two Truths.*

Sādhana The ritualized practice of worship and contemplation using the mandalas of tantric deities.

Samantabhadra The Primordial Buddha (Adibuddha). The Dharmakāya from which the Dzogchen teachings emanate.

Sambhogakāya The Enjoyment Body or Spiritual Rapture Body of Enlightened Awareness which appears with Five Certainties and is iconographically represented by the Five Buddha Families. This is the pure form-body of the Buddhas.

Saṃsāra Cyclic existence. A general term for the recurrent patterns of suffering, traditionally grouped into the six realms or lifestyles:

(1) gods
(2) demi-gods
(3) humans
(4) hungry spirits
(5) animals
(6) hell-beings

Saṅgha The community of like-minded people who adhere to the teachings of Lord Buddha.

Sanskṛit The major northern Indian literary language which gradually became the medium of expression for both Buddhist and Hindu philosophers up until the twelfth century when Moslems conquered India. Most of the original Buddhist scriptures now preserved in Tibetan texts were translated from Sanskṛit.

Sarma (gSar Ma, Tib.) The 'new' as opposed to the 'old' (sNying Ma) translations of Buddhist tantras from Sanskṛit sources. Sarma began with the translations of texts by Rinchen Zangpo and applies only to tantric scriptures.

Siddha Adept or Accomplished One. An esoteric practitioner who has achieved a high level of mystic accomplishment.

Siddhi The accomplishments and powers achieved through esoteric practices. See *Siddha.*

Skillful Means (Upāya, Skt.) Means employed to skillfully respond to any situation so as to help both oneself and other sentient beings by alleviating suffering and enhancing their growth toward complete Enlightenment. Such means can be supremely effective when employed in conjunction with Discriminating Wisdom (Prajñā, Skt.).

Śrāvaka Listeners. Pious listeners to Buddha's teachings, who follow the doctrine of Hinayana Buddhism.

Śrāvakayāna The vehicle or practice of the Śrāvaka, or Listeners.

Śūnyatā According to Mahāyāna doctrine, all phenomenal existence is inherently free from conceptualization in its true nature and is therefore empty or void of true existence.

Sūtra Discourses spoken by the Lord Buddha; one of the three collections (Tripiṭaka) of the Buddha's canonical teachings. See also *Tripiṭaka.*

Tantra Esoteric scriptures which are discourses on swift paths to Enlightenment. They include the Earlier Translated or Old Tantras and the Later Translated or New Tantras. See also *Sarma.*

Tantrayāna The Esoteric Vehicle. See *Mantrayāna.*

Tathatā An epithet for the natural, unfabricated and unchanging nature of ultimate, unconditional reality which is inherently free from all concepts.

Tenjur (bsTan 'Gyur, Tib.) The collected canonical commentaries of the writings of the Buddha. These were translated into Tibetan from Indian sources by Indian and Tibetan scholars.

Terton (gTer sTon, Tib.) Dharma Treasure Discoverer. Those special individuals who have been empowered and prophesied by Padmasambhava to discover and decode esoteric teachings hidden by him for the benefit of future generations.

Theravādin Literally, 'the Followers of the Elders'. The dominant form of Buddhism in Sri Lanka, Thailand, Burma and Laos. It belongs in the category of Hinayāna or southern Buddhism.

Thig Le (Tib.) Essence Drops. Subtle essence which moves within the human body, the understanding and control of which constitutes part of one's training in esoteric Buddhist practices and specifically in the attainment of Great Bliss.

Transmissions In the Dzogchen tradition, the teachings are communicated in three ways:

(1) Mind transmission: direct mind-to-mind transmission among the Buddhas.
(2) Indication transmission: transmission by signs among highly realized beings (Vidyadharas).
(3) Hearing transmission: verbal transmission from master to disciple.

Tranquility Meditation (Samatha, Skt.) Meditation whose purpose is the quieting and progressive focusing of the mind. It is necessary to practice this before attempting Insight Meditation.

Tripiṭaka Three Baskets. The three collections of the Buddha's canonical teachings:

(1) Sūtra—Collected discourses
(2) Vinaya—Collected teachings on rules of discipline
(3) Abhidharma—Collected teachings on metaphysics

Tsa Wu Ma (rTsa dBu Ma, Tib.) The central channel in the human body. To lead the energy (rLung) and mind into this central channel is one way of perfection of esoteric practice.

Tulku (sPrul sKu, Tib.) Due to the all-pervasive skill and compassion of Buddhahood, innumerable 'manifestations' of Enlightened Awareness continually occur in myriad forms—as bridges, works of art and in human form.

All serve to aid beings in easing their suffering and stimulating their quest for full Enlightenment.

In Tibet, Tulku is also a title given to rebirths of highly accomplished sages and scholars.

Tum-Mo (gTum Mo, Tib.) Heat-Yoga. Psychic Heat. One of the Six Yogas taught by the great Māropa and others as a means to generate the Great Bliss, the ultimate goal of tantric practice.

Two Truths Buddhist teachings recognize the necessity of comprehending reality (satya) from two viewpoints—the Absolute and the Relative. These are known as the Two Truths:

(1) Absolute Truth (Paramārthasatya, Skt.): reality apprehended

from the absolute or ultimate viewpoint, which comprehends the voidness (Śūnyatā) of all phenomena.

(2) Relative Truth (Saṁvṛtisatya, Skt.): reality apprehended from the relative viewpoint, which comprehends that all phenomena are dependently co-arisen (Pratītyasamutpāda, Skt.)

Vajra Vārāhī Diamond Sow. A sow-headed goddess, especially invoked to subdue ignorance.

Vajradhara (rDo rJe 'Chang, Tib.) A Saṃbhogakāya form of Buddhahood. In the Sarma or New Tantras of Tibet, Vajradhara is the most important figure and is the ultimate source of the esoteric teachings.

Vajrasattva (rDo rJe Sems dPa', Tib.) A Buddha in Sambhogakāya form taken as an object of meditation especially for the purification of defilements.

Vajrayāna The Adamantine Vehicle. The highest of the Three Vehicles or levels of practice in Buddhism. See also *Mantrayāna.*

Vinaya A collection of Lord Śākyamuni Buddha's teachings on proper moral conduct. See also *Tripiṭaka.*

Visualization Divinity (Dam Tshig Pa, Tib.) The visualized form of the deity in tantric meditative practices. See *Visualization Divinity.*

Wisdom Ḍākinī (mKha' 'Gro Ma, Tib.) Immortal, or enlightened goddesses.

Wisdom Divinity (Ye Shes Pa, Tib.) This is the actual deity which the meditator invites to come and dissolves into the visualized form of the deity in tantric meditative practices. See *Visualized Divinity.*

Wishing Gem A gem which fulfills or grants one's wishes. This symbolizes Buddha's Enlightened Mind, which is like a wishing jewel, because it grants all wishes.

Yāna Vehicle or Way. A coherent and consistent way of practicing the Buddha's teachings. Buddhism has been classified into two, three, four, six or nine Yānas according to different traditions. In the most popular sense, Buddhism is known nowadays in three categories of progressively faster paths of attainment: Hinayāna, Mahāyāna and Tantrayāna (or Vajrayāna).

Yānas of Cause The Mahāyāna is divided, according to Tibetan tradition, into the Yāna of Cause (Hetuyāna, Skt.) and Yāna of Result (Phalayāna, Skt.). The former is associated with the vehicle of perfection (Pāramaitāyāna) because the perfections act as stimuli or causes leading to spiritual fulfillment. The latter, the result vehicle, is the body of tantric teachings (Mantrayāna), because it uses the wisdom transmitted in initiations to perfect the attainment. Both of these are aspects of the Mahāyāna, hence their foundation is the cultivation of the Mind of Enlightenment (Bodhicitta).

Yoga Spiritual exercises or practices.

Yoga Śāstra Literary writings on mysticism. A category of esoteric teachings of Buddhism.

INDEX

MONASTERIES/TEMPLES

TEXTS/TANTRAS

PERSONS

GENERAL TERMS AND TEACHINGS

SCHOOLS AND LINEAGES